**With rebuttals, insults, and inappropriate asides
from the biggest names in Hollywood!**

"If he writes as well as he imitates me, you're in for a good time."
—ALBERT BROOKS

"Kevin Pollak is a mastermind of smart and funny. He attacks my funny bone the way a pit bull attacks my anklebone."
—STEVE MARTIN

"Kevin Pollak is one of those guys who shows up in every corner of the Business of Show—hit TV programs, award-winning movies, radio shows of every kind, and benefit dinners for worthy charities. I once saw him in the parking lot at Cirque du Soleil and hollered, 'Hey! Kevin!' but he didn't hear me. Like you, I wonder how he's made it to the Big Time. This book brings that mystery to a close."
—TOM HANKS

"Kevin Pollak does it all: He does impressions, he acts, he writes, he produces. He continues to impress with his unique and unabashed ability to use his friends' names for his sole benefit. A true Renaissance man."
—TOM CRUISE

"Unfortunately, as a personal favor, I allowed Leo Tolstoy a blurb calling *War and Peace* 'my most fun read ever.' That being the case, I am unable to say the same about *How I Slept My Way to the Middle*. Would that I had reserved that comment for Kevin Pollak, where the appraisal would be so much more deserved."
—JAMES L. BROOKS

"Unfortunately, I did a little digging, and Kevin Pollak's book was ghostwritten by a factory full of Chinese children hopped up on n-hexane. In spite of, or perhaps because of, that, I hear it's a great read."
—HARRY SHEARER

"Actor, writer, storyteller, stand-up, chat-show host, man about town, the most wonderful company, and now memoirist. Is there no end to his deranged ambition? Clearly not. I did two pictures with him and count myself lucky I got off with just two. A book I just couldn't wait to put down."
—GABRIEL BYRNE

How I Slept My Way to the Middle

Secrets and Stories from Stage, Screen, and Interwebs

KEVIN POLLAK

with Alan Goldsher

Lyons Press
Guilford, Connecticut
An imprint of Globe Pequot Press

Lyons Press is an imprint of Globe Pequot Press.

Project editor: Meredith Dias
Text design: Sheryl P. Kober
Layout: Joanna Beyer

Library of Congress Cataloging-in-Publication Data
Pollak, Kevin, 1958-
 How I slept my way to the middle : secrets and stories from stage,
screen, and interwebs / Kevin Pollak with Alan Goldsher.
  p. cm.
Includes index.
ISBN 978-0-7627-8055-6
1. Pollak, Kevin, 1958- 2. Actors—United States—Biography. 3.
Comedians—United States—Biography. I. Goldsher, Alan, 1966- II.
Title.
PN2287.P5715A3 2012
792.02'8092—dc23
[B]
                                                         2012018686

Printed in the United States of America

10 9 8 7 6 5 4 3 2 1

All photos contained in this book, aside from those with a specific credit line, are courtesy of the author's personal collection. Any failure to credit the appropriate photographer is unintentional and based on the author's memory rendered worthless by narcissism.

To Jaime Ann Fox, for igniting a new, brighter, warmer fire in my heart, mind, and under my ass.

You've heard it can be so very lonely at the top, but I know for a fact that it's fan-fucking-tastic in the middle.

CONTENTS

Contents

FOREWORD
by Penn Jillette

It's a pain in my ass that Kevin Pollak is funny. It makes him fun to have supper with, and he was good in our *Aristocrats* movie, telling dirty jokes—but it fucks up my dream. My dream is to have Kevin Pollak play Houdini.

Hey, Martin Luther King got his dream, what the fuck am I, chopped liver?

Kevin looks like Houdini. Kevin sounds like Houdini. (Kevin always sounds really lo-fi recorded on an Edison cylinder.) In the world I want to live in, Kevin is playing Houdini in a movie that isn't campy like Tony Curtis or jive-ass like that Broadway musical is going to be with Hugh Jackman playing Houdini.

Now, I love Hugh Jackman. He's been to our show, and he was fiercely nice and talented even backstage. In fact, he was more talented backstage than I am onstage. Hugh can sing and dance and everything, and his family is sweet and kind, and he's wicked good-looking.

So why the fuck is he playing Houdini?

Houdini didn't sing or dance, and he wasn't fucking good-looking.

This is why Kevin is perfect. Ugly-ass Kevin would be better than piece-of-ass Hugh.

Also, Hugh is Australian, and Houdini was so American that he was born in Budapest and pretended to be from Appleton, Wisconsin. Did Hugh ever claim to be from Wisconsin? Not that I know of, but what the fuck do I know?—I don't stalk Hugh's hot sexy ass. Kevin could claim to be from Wisconsin and not Frisco or whatever bullshit city he's from.

And if Hugh Jackman were from the USA, like Kevin is from the USA, I bet the assholes in his school would have called him Huge

Jack-off. Not because Hugh Jackman is a jackoff, but because his name sounds like that. Assholes do that; assholes make fun of your name even if it doesn't mean anything. I sure would have called him Huge Jack-off, and I bet Kevin would have too because Kevin's funny and Kevin can be an asshole, and you can bet your huge ackman that Houdini was an asshole.

Jackman is going to play Houdini in the Broadway show about Houdini, and the *New York Times* will write another great blowjob about him because he sings, dances, and eats pussy, and that shocks the *Times*. I can stop Kevin from singing and dancing . . . I'm way bigger than he is. I can't stop Hugh Jackman from dancing and singing because he has big Wolverine claws. Houdini didn't have big Wolverine claws. Kevin doesn't have big Wolverine claws, so why the fuck isn't Kevin playing Houdini?

There's an intensity to Kevin that he covers up in his stupid stand-up act. If Kevin weren't funny, we would be more likely to see that focus, playing Houdini. Kevin would be a great Houdini. A non-dancing, non-singing, not funny, not jack-off Houdini. Kevin's name doesn't sound like Jack-off, but . . . don't bring up Polish jokes or short jokes with the little fellow, whose name sounds a lot like "Polack." I bet assholes called him Polack, but I bet Hugh Jackman never called Kevin "Polack" because Hugh is a gentleman.

Houdini was a pure little fireplug of intensity. Who knows?—maybe Houdini did the first Shatner that every other two-bit piece-of-shit comic rips off. How would I know?

I think Kevin would be great as Houdini, so let's have him star in a serious movie about Houdini, OK? You know, there hasn't been a good Houdini movie. Harvey Keitel sure was good as Houdini—and I bet assholes made fun of the name "Harvey," don't you think? It's kind of a goofy name—in that shitty movie about fairies. But that doesn't count because the movie was shitty. Was Harvey better than Kevin (the Polack) would be? I don't know, but Harvey didn't ask me to write jack shit for his book, and he was in *The Piano*, and that sure blew.

I wonder if Kevin would be naked in his Houdini movie like Harvey was in *The Piano*. Houdini stripped during his escapes, so naked wouldn't be completely gratuitous, but I love gratuitous nudity anyway. I'd like to see Kevin's cock playing Houdini's cock. But I'd probably rather see Huge Jack-off's cock for lots of obvious reasons.

Anyway, Houdini died at fifty-two, and Kevin is fifty-five now, so *tick tock tick tock*, people. Let's get this movie fucking made. Kevin will be great. Let's all work together and make Penn's dream come true and let Kevin play Houdini. Is that too much to ask? I mean, that and a cure for AIDS with the patent in my name and an eleven-inch dick . . . like Huge Jack-off's.

I bet that's why he got the part.

MORE FOREWORD

by Billy Bob Thornton

Years ago, a producer friend of mine left me a message saying Kevin Pollak wanted to meet me because he was a big fan and that maybe we could do something together. I was thrilled because I was a big fan and would shit myself to work with him.

I called Kevin, and we had a short but nice ass-kissing festival on the phone. I'd seen him interviewed, and the voice didn't quite match up with the voice I'd heard so many times—much thinner and kind of squirrelly—and I actually said to him that his voice sounded different on the phone.

"You think that sounds different, listen to this," he said. Then he proceeded to do an impression of Alan Arkin for about five excruciating minutes. I was confused, but you know how eccentric Hollywood types are, so I just chalked it up as that. Plus I figured it would make a good story to tell my friends, and if he gave me a job, I didn't give a shit if he did half an hour of Woody Woodpecker.

When I said, "I actually know your daughter Rebecca. I had several pitch meetings with her when she worked at MGM/UA," he started laughing and said, "I knew you'd be a wise guy in person. That's funny shit."

Anyway, we set up a lunch, and I said wherever you want to go is fine by me, expecting to get a nice free business lunch at whatever fancy place he frequented that had his name on some kind of spaghetti or whatever—Fettuccine Pollak or something. He told me to meet him at Koo Koo Roo chicken over on Beverly and Larchmont. OK, no fancy lunch, he's a regular guy. That's good. Job's in the bag.

I went there to meet him, didn't see him right away, and then this short guy who I vaguely recognized came up and said, "Billy? Kevin Pollak."

Long story short of course is: I don't listen very well, and I'm not too thorough about details, and I thought that I was meeting great film director Sydney Pollack.

You can imagine my disappointment. No big movie job, just some needy comic who probably wanted a job from me. Which, it turns out, he did.

One way or the other, it's not so bad hanging out with him all these years. He makes me look like Cary Grant. Other than one case of chlamydia I got one of those nights when I got the better-looking chick, it's worked out pretty well.

INTRODUCTION
Howard Hughes and Logorrhea

It's a warm, sunny Wednesday afternoon in Los Angeles, smack-dab in the midsummer of 1994. I'm sitting on my ass in my trailer, waiting to continue work on a little heist film called *The Usual Suspects*. (Yes, thank you. Please be seated, really.) My then-exciting clamshell cell phone announces a call from my agent, who quickly moves past the niceties with The News: "There's an offer from Martin Scorsese."

"Holy shit, really? I guess I can die a happy man now."

"Well," he says, "you may want to do the movie first."

"You're probably right. Tell me more."

"It's called *Casino*. Nick Pileggi, the guy who wrote *Goodfellas*, wrote it—"

"Holy fuck!" I shout.

"Couldn't agree more. And it takes place in Vegas—"

"*Holy fuck!*"

"Robert De Niro and Joe Pesci are playing the leads."

"HOLY FUCK," I shout, even louder, scaring the shit out of my *Suspects* costar Gabriel Byrne, holed up in his trailer all the way down the street.

My agent says he's already messengered the script to the set, then adds, "It's mesmerizing." No surprise there. Any film fan worth a damn knows that Nick Pileggi is a genius of gangsterism. Also, let's be honest: It only half matters what's on the pages of that script when Mr. Scorsese is at the helm because there's no way any reader will ever be able to see the divine magic he sees. If a screen direction reads, "Exterior: A chicken crosses the road," you and I see a chicken crossing a road in anticipation of a joke or a fast-moving truck. Scorsese sees a breathtaking cinematic journey of the Mafia's bloody takeover of every KFC franchise from Bayonne to Schenectady.

I tell my wonderful agent, George, that I don't need to read the script. "I'm in."

He pauses, which instantly registers on my "uh-oh" indicator. Then he says, "Like I said, it's a definite offer . . ."

"You're not going to say 'but,' are you?" I grumble.

"No, it's an offer. Period. It's just . . . well, it's a long-standing tradition between Scorsese and De Niro that, if you're going to play an important role in one of their films, you have to go meet them individually. They each like to say hello."

"That tells me that, if the meetings don't go well, the offer is rescinded."

"No, it's a formality. But it's also an important tradition they have."

"George, there's only one reason to have a sit-down like this, let alone two of them, and you know this 'offer' is only good as long as I get through this important ritual."

We both know that I've always been happy to meet with anybody to get a role, and if it means a chance to work with the great Scorsese, I'd sleep with whomever His Geniusness would like me to. The part that I was being "offered" was of Phillip Green, the mob's extremely well-tailored, overly manicured, über–clean-cut front man, who on paper would be in charge of a new $60 million (1970s millions) casino in Vegas called The Tangiers.

The sudden nausea I'm feeling stems from the unfortunate timing of their requests for a sit-down. As George runs down the details of the aforementioned ritual meetings, I stare at the mirror before me and, *man*, I am not Phillip Green material.

My part in *The Usual Suspects* demands that I look like a sociopathic thief, killer, and weapons expert—albeit a lovable and quick-witted sociopath, to be fair. The version of me in the mirror during this magical Scorsese-offer life moment looks disheveled and more than a little nuts. My hair—then full and curly, unlike now—is as unkempt as it has ever been. A healthy goatee surrounded by a serious ten o'clock shadow covers my face. This won't jibe with the look for my theoretical *Casino* character: slick, clean-shaven, and not at all nuts.

But, as George explains, I have no choice. I've been cleared from work, and the following day I'm scheduled to meet with Academy Award–winner Robert De Niro in a lavish bungalow at the absurdly luxurious Bel-Air Hotel.

The next morning, as I'm getting ready to head over, I decide to bring along an 8x10 headshot to demonstrate that I clean up nice. My plan is to knock on De Niro's door, and then when he opens up, I'll hold the photo over my face so he can see the real me and understand that, despite my current state of shagginess, I can look the part. *Plus*, I think, *the gag might even make him smile, which won't be the worst way to begin this all-important, wildly-nerve-wracking-for-one-of-us ritualistic sit.*

I arrive at the Bel-Air, where for a mere $27 you too can have your car parked by a handsome young yet-to-be-cast movie star of tomorrow. Ellen Lewis, Scorsese's wonderfully sweet casting director, takes me inside to the expansive lobby, where I'm seated with another *Casino*-"offered" actor waiting to meet De Niro. This particular actor proceeds to cut into my unsightly facial hair with the precision of a Jedi knight. But this isn't just any actor—it's Don Rickles, whose razor-sharp barbs send me into much-needed hysterics.

Ellen leaves us to check on the great Bobby D., which affords Rickles a moment to fawn quietly over my acting in Barry Levinson's *Avalon* and Rob Reiner's *A Few Good Men*. I thank him and insist, sincerely, that when I saw his dramatic turn in *Kelly's Heroes* it was the first moment I believed it possible that one day I could get a shot at such a lofty opportunity.

He thanks me, then describes how excited he is to rip into De Niro, sending me into another laughing fit.

"Aren't you even a little nervous to meet him today?" I ask.

"Kid, De Niro loves me."

"Everyone loves you, Don."

"Yeah, yeah, I know, I know, but listen: I just found out that when De Niro was a kid growing up in New York, there were two types of groups hanging out on the street corners. There were the doo-wop groups, who stood in a circle and sang songs, and there were the put-down groups, who stood in a circle and said, 'Your mother this, and your mother that.' Believe it or not, De Niro—shy, demure De Niro—was in a put-down group! Anyway, I find out that all those kids in De Niro's group grew up thinking I was some kind of god. No kidding. I'm gonna rip him a new one big enough to park a Cadillac in."

Spoiler alert #1: He did—and it was beyond anything you could imagine. Much more about this later.

Ellen rejoins us. "Kevin, it's time."

She might as well have said, "Kevin, what would you like as your last meal?" because it felt like I was heading to the chair.

As she walks me to De Niro's tucked-away bungalow, she says, "Bobby's harmless. There's nothing to worry about."

Who the hell says, "There's nothing to worry about" when there's actually nothing to worry about?

Suddenly it hits me: All I have to do to survive this meeting is to say as little as possible. *He just wants to make sure I'm not a kiss-ass or an asshole. I'll be neither! I'll be respectful and speak only when spoken to.* I remember some advice that my Aunt Shirley Zucker bestowed upon me when I was a preteen: "Sometimes you shouldn't try so hard to entertain. Sometimes you should dummy up."

Dummy up . . . dummy up . . . dummy up, I tell myself as Ellen knocks on HIS door, pats my arm, and strolls away.

I look at the headshot in my hand and wonder if I should abandon this now-certainly-stupid sight-gag prop, but before I can decide whether to use it the door opens, and standing in the threshold I don't see the Robert De Niro you and I know. Hell, I don't see Travis Bickle or Jake LaMotta or Al Capone or Max Cady or even a young Vito Corleone.

I see Howard Hughes.

And not the young, dashing Howard Hughes. We're talking the last-six-months-of-his-life Howard Hughes: long gray hair, straggly gray beard, well-worn black bathrobe, mismatched pajamas. The only things missing are the five-inch fingernails and Kleenex boxes on his feet.

I'm instantly freaked out, and before you can say "What were you thinking, Kevin?" I throw the 8x10 of my stupid face into the bushes in front of De Niro's $5,000-a-night Bel-Air bungalow. An easy decision really, given what was standing before me. I mean, for me to hold up a professional portrait, then point to my shaggy face and say, "I don't normally look this way" in front of deathbed Howard Hughes is the very definition of absurd.

"Come on in," he says, then heads back inside the massive suite. Even though it's mid-morning, the curtains are drawn—and these are *heavy* curtains, mind you, hotel-grade blackout curtains. If it wasn't for the lone reading lamp illuminating a huge, aged-leather easy chair, I wouldn't have been able to see a thing.

He gestures at a sofa-like chair on one side of the room, then plops down in his and asks me, "Can I get you anything?"

I sit down. "No, thank you. I'm fine."

He looks around the dark room with that squished up, squinted De Niro half smile–half frown face of his. "So, how ya doin'?"

"I'm fine."

"Great. Can I get you anything?"

"No, thanks. Thank you."

"Okay." *Pause.* "Great." *Pause.* "So." *Pause.* "I just wanted to say hello." *Pause.* "Wanted to meet you, ya know."

Long pause.

"Sure I can't get you anything?"

"Very kind of you," I say, "but I honestly can't think of anything."

"Ok, sure." *Pause.* "Terrific." *Pause.* "Hmm." *Pause.* "Just . . ." *Pause.* "Wanted to meet you."

Long pause.

"Ya doin' all right?"

"Oh, yes," I say. "Thank you, yes."

We go through that painful routine three more times, and in between each exchange there's a full minute of silence, during which time he continues to look around the dark room. The whole time, I'm thinking, *Do not say a fucking thing, Pollak. The only way for you to blow this is to speak. Just keep your mouth shut.* Not speaking was proving to be a problem, though, as De Niro wasn't saying a whole hell of a lot either, and when you have a conversation, *somebody* should talk. But I would be damned if somehow I was going to end up saying the wrong thing. If he thought me odd because of my respectful silence and this once-in-a-lifetime opportunity evaporated due to my zipped lip, then so be it.

Several interminable minutes of awkward silence later—interspersed with him asking if I wanted anything—he reiterates, "I just wanted to meet you, and say hello, and, and, and, meet you. You met with Marty yet?"

"No, I'm meeting him tomorrow."

"Great. Sure I can't get you anything?"

"I'm fine, thanks."

Then it dawns on me that my own lack of sparkling conversation might be contributing to the discomfort, so I try to come up with something clever to say . . .

"*This is a lovely bungalow*"?

Nope.

"*Is this ridiculous look of yours for a movie?*"?

Nope.

"*I brought an 8x10 to explain why I look the way I do, but you, on the other hand, look like the Elephant Man for reasons I am not able to discern.*"?

Nope.

I can't come up with anything, so I keep quiet.

Eventually he asks me if I want anything, and I'm *this* close to saying, "You know what, *Bob?*—and I understand that you like to be called Bob, but I'll never call you Bob because I'll never be comfortable with you—I'd like a salad from room service, but I'm not going to ask you to order me one because it would mean another forty-five minutes of this torturous, hellish meeting." But wisely I keep my lip zipped.

Finally, finally, finally, the moment I've been praying for arrives: He stands up. As I rise in deference, he says: "I just wanted to meet you and say hello." It took all of my strength to keep from saying, "Let me get this straight: You just wanted to meet me and say hello. Is that right?"

After another pause, he adds, "I look forward to working with you."

"It will be an honor, sir," I say as he ushers me to the door.

You fucking moron! I think in the hallway. *Why did you say, "It will be an honor"? Why did you call him "sir"? You came off like a little sycophant. You blew it!* With all of that running through my overtaxed brain, I almost crash into Ellen Lewis.

"How'd it go?" she smiles.

"Horribly."

She nods. "That's exactly how it goes for everybody."

"How do you know?"

"Let me tell you what happened," she says. "You sat down, then he said, 'Can I get you anything?', then you said, 'No, thank you,' then he said, 'I just wanted to meet you and say hello,' then you went through that routine three, maybe four more times."

"Actually it was seven."

She nods, then calls to Rickles, "OK, Don. Go on in."

Rickles wanders over, thanks Ellen, and asks me, "How'd it go, kid?"

I give him my most sincere smile and say, "Don, I've never had so much fun talking to somebody in my entire life. Nicest guy you'll ever meet. Wouldn't shut up. Zero inner monologue."

"Nice try, kid. Ellen already told me the deal. See you in Vegas."

Two days later, I am granted an audience with the masterful auteur Martin Scorsese. We meet in his trailer on the set of something he's shooting, and it's the exact opposite of the De Niro sit. No *Can I get you anythings*. No *I just wanted to meet yous*. No Kleenex boxes. Just a brilliant dissertation on the history of film. The only similarity between the two meetings—one of which lasts seven minutes, and one of which lasts approximately forever—is that in each one I say about twelve words.

Marty never sat down. Marty never stopped moving. Marty never stopped talking. It was truly astonishing to watch. I don't recall ever being so worthless to a conversation in my life. I remember at one point actually thinking, *Thank God he doesn't need me to contribute because I can't possibly keep up with whatever the hell he's talking about.* Every third sentence had a movie reference in it that I didn't get: "That scene in act one is going to be just like that scene in *The Dark Horse.* You ever see *The Dark Horse*?"

"I'm sorry, no."

"1932. Alfred Green. Terrific picture. Anyhow, it's gonna be just like that scene at the beginning of the film. But also kinda like *Quicksand*, 1923, Howard Hawks wrote it, Jack Conway directed. You see it?"

"Um, no."

"Great film, great film. I'll get you a print. Directly influenced *Daughter of Deceit.* Buñuel, 1951. You see it?"

"Gosh, no."

"Underappreciated masterpiece. Guy's a genius. Huge influence on . . ."

And so on.

I'm dizzy, enchanted, and frightened, but mostly I feel like I should keep my mouth shut because if I don't say the wrong thing then the offer is still good, and I'll do *Casino.*

Finally he asks me, "How'd it go with Bob? Did he sit there and say nothing?"

"You know, Kevin, the first picture to win the Oscar was called *Wings*. Great picture, great. Terrific footage of actual biplanes dogfighting . . . well, they were doing war games, but gorgeous stuff, really. You ever see it?" Um, no.

"He was . . . delightful."

Nodding knowingly, Marty says, "Yeah, he doesn't say much, does he?"

"No he doesn't, sir." I smile as he launches into a riff about Las Vegas films.

How does this guy get any work done, considering his inability to stop talking? Holy shit, what if this is never going to end? What if I have to spend the rest of my life in this trailer? What if I'm being verbally kidnapped?

One hour and thirty-seven minutes later, an assistant director who needed him on set negotiates my release. I'm older but somehow not wiser, my goatee is longer, my mind is blown—and I have the part.

How I Slept My Way to the Middle

1

Cos and the Zuckers

I'm obsessed with comedy albums, always have been. *Obsessed.* Many a reporter will learn this and ask for my favorite. "Oh, man, you're fucked," I always tell him. "I can't possibly pick a single favorite." Then I reel off a list of records that each and every one of you should own: Albert Brooks's *Comedy Minus One,* George Carlin's *Class Clown,* Woody Allen's double album on Fantasy Records, and David Frye's *Richard Nixon,* among others.

But, like they say, you never forget your first.

It's 1967. I'm ten when my mother, Elayne—spelled Elaine until she changed it in her forties—brings home the album *Bill Cosby Is a Very Funny Fellow . . . Right!,* then tells me, "We're going to listen to this right now." ("Why did she change the spelling of her name?" you may ask. Because she's nuts, party of one.) She herds me, my father, Bob, and my older brother, Craig, into the living room so we can listen to it on the stereo/hi-fi.

Now, you may think that you know what a stereo/hi-fi is, but I'm here to tell you that you don't. First and foremost, it's a piece of furniture. It measures seven feet across and four feet high. For perspective, put your iPod Nano next to a Honda Accord, and you can see how far we've come. It's all wood—walnut, to be specific—the mesh-covered speakers are built into either side, and a lift-top in the middle covers the turntable. When my mother drops the needle onto the record, a voice that will change my life forever emerges from the furniture:

> *I am not from New York City. I was born in Philadelphia, raised in Philadelphia, educated in Philadelphia. For those of you that plan to come into New York anytime soon, don't bring a lot of money with you. It's the greatest city in the world, and you can*

get all the entertainment you want for only 15 cents. Ride any of the subway trains they have out here. It's marvelous. Not only will they take you where you want to go, and bring you back, but they go out of their way to entertain you. They put a nut in every car.

At first, I giggle at the voice coming from the furniture, but then I grow unnerved as I watch my parents laugh uncontrollably. I'd seen them laugh with their friends at parties, and they often chuckled at something that Craig or I did, but this is different. It's a powerful moment, and it makes an adhesive connection in my brain: *Comedy albums make my parents laugh uncontrollably.* But at the same time it's frightening because this laughter—this involuntary laughter—is as intense as if they were sobbing, and this bizarre behavior freaks me out. It's that foreign, that weird, that worrisome.

Are Mom and Dad gonna be all right?

Now, I had contracted a lifelong illness four or five years earlier called, Hey-Look-at-Me Disease. (HLAMD is no smirking matter. One of the symptoms is singing and dancing in front of the jukebox in my grandfather's bar; performances like that eventually result in signing my first autograph at age six, but we'll get to that.) So minutes after I see Mom and Dad break down laughing, it all crystallizes . . .

I want to be the voice in the furniture that makes Mom and Dad laugh like this.

One small snag: I have no idea what a stand-up comedian is. For that matter, I don't really know what a comedian is. To me, Jackie Gleason or the Marx Brothers are just guys on television or in the movies who make me laugh. There's nobody around to help me figure out what these mirth-makers are all about. Like a ten-year-old Lewis and/or Clark, I must discover utterly new, untold lands for myself. While no one else is around.

The next day, when I come home, Dad's at work, Mom's out, and Craig's still at school. With nobody in the house, I go into the living room, pick up the Cosby album, open the top of the furniture, and gently place the record onto the turntable. Yes, oh yes, I'm quite aware that if anything should happen to this priceless vinyl disc, I'm grounded for the rest of my life with no food or water. But like an instant junkie, I gotsta gets me some *RIGHT NOW.* I'm thrilled that nobody's around because, for the first time in my life, I want to experience a form of entertainment alone. I want it to be my secret, a hideout in my life from the others who can't possibly appreciate this as much as I do. And I'm about to appreciate it again. And again. And again.

This goes on literally for weeks, and it organically evolves to another level. Like any genuine addict, I need a new version of this drug, a better, more intense high from the storytelling coming from the furniture. I can't sit idly by while this world-altering experience is happening. I've got to . . . stand up.

By now, I've heard the album one hundred times—I memorize it without knowing why or how—and am doing what I find out later is called lip-synching. It's not a conscious decision. I never think, *I should stand up in front of the stereo and act like the man telling the stories.* It's not considered, this game I'm playing—it just happens.

He speaks with a musical rhythm, this Bill Cosby, but there's also a sense of calm. There's no *rat-a-tat-tat* to his delivery, just the rhythm of the story. Little do I know, I'm learning the single most important aspect of any form or style of comedy, and that's timing. Also, little do I realize how insanely fortunate I am to be conducting said studies at the aural feet of a true master. I subconsciously learn pure comedy rhythm when Bill takes a pause, or clears his throat, or takes a breath during one of his stories—not by accident or happenstance but rather as a carefully calculated way of getting the most laughs out of a particular moment in the story. The man has discovered after many, many performances that, if he purposely clears his throat at that *precise* second in the routine, the audience is guaranteed to laugh. Remember, though, I'm not stopping each time after I learn one of these little nuances of his performance to consider the value or potential of his calculations; I'm just a child playing along. There are no interactive games in 1967.

This is the most fun I've ever had in my young life, and I have no idea why or even what the hell is happening.

Eventually, I begin doing gestures with my hands, although I'm not at all concerned if my gestures match what I imagine are his. All I have is his voice, and that's enough for me to create the whole physical world of those tales, like that of Noah:

> *There's a fella by the name of Noah. He built an ark. Everybody knows he built an ark. If somebody says, "What'd Noah do?" you'd say, "Well, he built an ark." But very few people know about the conversation (*clears throat*) that went on between the Lord and Noah. You see, Noah was in his rec room, sawing away, making a few things for the home; he was a good carpenter.* VOO-PAH, VOO-PAH, VOO-PAH, VOO-PAH, DING.
>
> *"Noah?"*
> *"Did somebody call?"*
> VOO-PAH, VOO-PAH, VOO-PAH, DING.
> *"Noah!"*
> *"Who is that?"*
> *"It's the Lord, Noah!"*
> *"Riiiiiight!"*

Like any intoxicant, the further I fall down the rabbit hole of the lip-synching game, the more I can't wait to get home and stand up in front of the imaginary audience that hangs on my routine. I've graduated to performer. I'm no longer playing or even learning the material so that I might make my parents laugh. Now I'm racing home to work on The Act.

I've taken ownership of what I'm doing, and when I stand in the living room to perform, I imagine that the audience laughing on the album is *my* audience. I can actually see them seated in front of me. The ritual becomes so intense, private, and potent that when Mom finally discovers me lip-synching in front of the furniture, it's like she caught me masturbating. Fortunately, she never actually caught me masturbating—although she did come home early when I was losing my virginity in my bedroom with senior year classmate Julie Lewis, causing the quickest exit from inside a woman known to history.

Yes, I checked the records before claiming that. What the hell kind of book do you think I'm writing here?

A Few Good Words from Kevin's Mom

When Kevin was twelve, I remember watching him at an audition. He was doing a great job, and I asked one of my friends, "I wonder where Kevin gets it from?" She said, "You." I said, "Really?" because I never thought I was funny. But I do remember when Kevin had his friends over, once in a while, I'd put on a Cosby record and put on a little show for them with some dancing and miming. I didn't tell jokes, though. Kevin is the joke teller.

As usual, at that point in my ritual, I'm facing away from the furniture, focused on my audience and gauging their mood tonight, so I don't know how long my mother has been in the room before she laughs.

My heart stops.

I take the needle off the record and spin around, as ashamed as I would be if my pants were at my ankles and my hand was working its magic. I'm so horrified that all I think to say is what's in my young heart: "I'm sorry, I'm *really* sorry, I'm sorry."

After she regains control of herself, an odd look comes over her face, which I later learn is called a lightbulb moment, and she says: "You have to do that for the Zuckers at Passover."

"OK," I say immediately. I mean, why not? My secret's out. There's a sense of relief and celebration. If Mom thinks I'm ready for the big leagues, then let's do this.

Before I get anywhere near my first audience, she explains what lip-synching is and blows my mind.

"Other people stand in front of the stereo and do what I'm doing?"

"Sure. What, you think you're the first person to realize that this is funny?"

I remember reading somewhere that Jerry Lewis started his career lip-synching Danny Kaye albums. Later I'd have the opportunity to ask him about it. (Yeah, another story we'll get to in a bit.)

So according to Mom, I'm legit. I have what's called an "act," and she's going to make a call and get me my first booking. Of course, she doesn't phrase any of it that way. She's not a stage mom. I really want to be clear about this because you could easily misconstrue that she pushed me into performing, that she manipulated my playtime into an act. Showing off for the family was her idea; the career in showbiz was mine.

The Zuckers' Passover get-together is always part feast and part family reunion. Like a lot of extended Jewish families of the day, there are about forty of us at the seder. There's Uncle Sid, who can turn a cloth napkin into an adorable rabbit that darts up his arm in the blink of an eye, a trick that he taught me and a trick that I still perform for children and adults with the same marvelous results to this day. My Uncle Sylvan, patriarch of the Zucker clan, at whose house we're all gathered, tends bar like the happiest man on the planet and tells the best jokes anyone present has ever heard. Oh, look, over in the corner, it's Aunt Bessie, bless her, for whom every year my mom insists on buying a new dress, only to have her ask, "Does this make me look fat?" (It takes me until the age of nineteen to answer Aunt Bessie honestly: "You want to know what makes you look fat, Aunt Bessie? *Vision.* The fact that we can *see.*") There's cousin Terry, who a few years before took me to see the Dave Clark Five, after which I signed my first autograph at age six—a historic moment soon to be discussed.

Given all the talent in the room, you'd think that I'd be nervous. After all, save for a select few who'd seen me putzin' around in front of the jukebox at my grandfather's bar, none of this crowd has ever seen me perform. But there I am, perched on the raised white-painted brick hearth attached to the front of the white-painted brick fireplace in the living room, cool as can be. Since the Zuckers' living room seated only seventeen, we're looking at a standing-room-only gig.

I tackle all three parts of the Noah trilogy—three minutes each, nine minutes total—and my performance is an instant hit. The whole family won't shut up about my being a natural performer, and they're each taking turns claiming that they're the one who *knows* I'm gonna be a star one day. Me? I'm a ten-year-old who doesn't appreciate being condescended to, and I just want to know which one of them wants to bankroll my first tour.

With my HLAMD in full bloom, it's inevitable that I bring the album to school for Show and Tell. After I do the routine for the class, my teacher freaks out and says, "You need to do this for the entire school." Who was I to refuse? She's clearly got taste and an eye on my future. The following Friday, I stand onstage in front of all the sixth, seventh, and eighth graders at John Muir Middle School, next to a little record player hooked up to the auditorium's PA system, lip-synching Bill Cosby's "Noah and the Ark" routine.

In front of almost a thousand kids.

Can you guess what the single best aspect of all this newfound attention from my fellow students is?

Go ahead. Formulate an educated guess.

Seriously, go on. I'm curious how many of you get it right.

Oh. We have a way of finding out, never you mind how . . .

OK, all of you who guessed that the answer is girls have won a free gift. The rest of you now know the true reason that 84 percent of all males (girls are more mature than boys, duh) pursue a life in the performing arts beyond just fuckin' around on picnic benches in the park after teen club dances.

For the first time in my life, multiple girls pay attention to me—all at the same time!—and I *cannot believe this is happening.* I mean, how does this not get taught to every boy? Sure, later, in high school, I evolved into being the smart, funny friend whom the girls I desired all wanted to come to and cry about the boy of their dreams. But at eleven years old, I was the bee's knees, muthafucka.

The following year, I use Cosby's Noah as an audition piece to get a starring role in a local theater's production of a musical called *A Twist of Wry. Wry* is about a thirteen-year-old Jewish boy and his family's preparations for his bar mitzvah. It's being directed by a temperamental, flamboyant, demonstrative, frightening-as-hell man who, I realize much later, is a flaming homosexual. At the time, though, I think he's a few weeks shy of a straitjacket and a rubber room.

It's during the brief run of this *brilliant* community theater production that I have my first off-set romance with the only Jewish girl I ever dated, Michelle Freiberg. It's a white-hot thrill ride that haunts my dreams to this day. I seem to recall it ended abruptly when I made a premature attempt for second base.

Women mature faster than boys, my eye.

A Few Good Words from Kevin's Mom

That man who directed *A Twist of Wry* was a small fish in a smaller fishbowl, and he acted like he was directing a Broadway play. But I was excited beyond belief because Kevin seemed so at home up there. I've never been nervous for him. How could I be nervous? He took command of the stage! This started inside the womb, and he came out already prepared for show business. As a matter of fact, he probably did a couple minutes of stand-up for the doctor.

For the next six years, I do my Cosby album lip-synch act anywhere and everywhere I can: the school's annual talent show, the school's annual Fold Festival, the school's Daddy/Daughter Dinner and Dance (yes, a real thing), and eventually at my first paid gig at the Elks Club. I never once think about uttering a word, or writing my own act, or doing an impersonation, but I don't have to because every time anyone sees the sight of a precocious little Jewish kid lip-synching to Bill Cosby, it kills 100 percent of the time. This act is all I'll ever have to do, right?

Right.

It's around this time that I discover what a comedian looks like when he tells his stories.

"*Heeeeeeeeeeeeeere's Johnny!*"

Postscript (or Prescript, I suppose)

I was actually prepared to be in the spotlight from the age of five.

It's 1963, I'm six years old, and in San Jose, California, the Dave Clark Five are almost neck-and-neck with the Beatles. I listen to their album until the needle can't advance because the grooves in the vinyl are too deep.

The DC5 has a gig at the Circle Star Theater—an in-the-round venue that will play a large part in our story in mere moments—and my thirteen-year-old cousin Terry Zucker knows I'm obsessed, so she gets us two tickets, and I freak out. What a first concert!

Sonny and Cher, fur vests and all, are the opening act (!!!!), followed by Dave Clark's group, who, while clearly not true music geniuses like the members of the Fab Four, are a wildly adored band who, like the Beatles, have to go to eleven in order to be heard over nonstop screams. In the midst of all this, Terry shouts into my ear, "After the show, we'll go to the side stage door, wait until they come out, and get their autographs."

Oh my God. I'm gonna meet the Dave Clark Five. Is this real? What if I meet just the other four, but not The Dave Clark? You know what? Doesn't matter.

They finish up, and we go to the stage door and run into a gaggle of thirteen-year-old girls. I'm the only boy. Not just the only six-year-old boy. <u>The only boy.</u>

Every few seconds, I turn to Terry and ask, "When're they coming out? When're they coming out? When're they coming out? Seriously, <u>when're</u> they coming out?" I'm an unbelievable pain in the ass.

Disillusioned after forty-five minutes, Terry has her own lightbulb moment that will change the course of history. She checks out the lay of the land. She notices the stairs leading up to the side stage door. At the top of the stairs, there's a little platform. Terry points up to the platform. "Kevin, while we wait for them to come out . . . well, you've got their songs memorized. Why don't you go up there and—"

Before she finishes, I'm at the top of the stairs, on the platform, belting out, "Catch us if you can, ooooooh-ooh-ooh. Catch us if you ca-an, ooooooh, ooh-ooh," bobbing back and forth like a lunatic spawn who thinks he's The Dave Clark.

I sing another five songs, and those thirteen-year-old girls are once again screaming . . . but they're screaming for me! (Not likely because I was such a wonderful singer. They probably thought I was cute. Plus they were bored to fucking tears.)

After I finish, one of these girls takes her autograph book—which she's been clutching for hours—and shoves it in my face. After all, she had to get <u>somebody's</u> autograph. As I'm signing, a few more of the girls line up to get their Kev Hancock.

But here's the thing: I'm six. I haven't been taught how to write in cursive yet, so I had to print my name. While I signed, er, printed those autographs, those thirteen-year-old girls giggled and smiled at me, and I was done. There was no turning back. All I'd done was memorize the words to my favorite . . .

Wait a sec.

Hmm.

Now there's an idea . . .

2

The Plane to Showbiz

Throughout my life—kidhood, adulthood, and everywhere in between-hood—I've done some nervy, ballsy things that, today, I often explain as taking life by the reins and creating my own destiny. In other words, I've done some crazy shit, and it paid off beyond any conceivable expectations.

One of my earliest nutty moves happens when I'm seventeen. I buy tickets to see master impressionist Rich Little at the Circle Star Theater, a revered venue in San Carlos, just south of San Francisco, the city of my birth, and thirty minutes north of San Jose, where I still lived with my parents. The Circle Star is famous for having a revolving stage that's conducive to almost nothing. Still, it was a big part of my young life, as witnessed by the infamous Dave Clark Five autograph session.

At that point, I'd been working on impersonations of Marlon Brando, Cary Grant, President Nixon, and Peter Falk's Lieutenant Columbo, among others, for the previous couple of years. After seeing Rich Little perform on *The Tonight Show,* I know that, when it comes to impersonating celebrity voices, Rich Little is beyond *The Man.* David Frye's *Nixon* album is truly brilliant, and Frank Gorshin and Godfrey Cambridge have small stables of famous voices they could do well, as did John Byner—but Little has no equal, and he's an enormous influence on my early work.

For example, one of my favorite voices to emulate is Johnny Carson, but, even though I'm a *Tonight Show* fanatic, the basis of my impression comes not from Johnny himself, but from Rich.

> Dana Carvey, who came up the comedy ranks in San Francisco at the same time I did—and who does a mean Carson himself—also used Rich Little's Johnny as his template. So in a sense,

Robin Williams, Mike Pritchard, Dana Carvey, Alex Bennett, me, and Jerry Seinfeld, cracking wise in San Francisco, circa 1984.

at the beginning of our careers, we were both impersonating Rich Little impersonating Carson. Ask anyone who does solid impersonations, and they will acknowledge someone else as being the one who cracked it first. Even my William Shatner impression, which became the template for countless other Shatners, was inspired by seeing John Belushi's version on *Saturday Night Live*. Even though, when you Google "Christopher Walken impersonation," my name comes up on top, the first guy I saw do Walken was Jay Mohr. While I was honing my Walken, I begged Jay for helpful tips, to which he said, "When doing Walken, every one-syllable word, becomes a two-syllable word. Like 'no' becomes 'No-oh.'" I remember hearing Jay mention on the great Sirius radio show *Opie and Anthony* that his Walken was inspired by a comic named Roger Kabler.

Anyway, Rich Little's gig at the Circle Star Theater is my first live comedy show—and I'm excited beyond words—but I use the word "comedy" here loosely because Rich Little wasn't known as a hilarious comedian. Even at seventeen, I realize that the man is a brilliant technician, but his routines . . . not so much. His lack of material inspires me to perfect a few jokes of my own. Humor or lack thereof aside, Rich is a hero, and weeks before I attend his show I decide that I need my hero to glimpse my talent somehow. Suddenly, it's absolutely *crucial* that he learn of my existence.

The question becomes: How? How am I going to show the great and powerful Rich Little that I'm talented? Then, as is the case with many of my nerviest, ballsiest moves, the answer comes to me out of the ozone.

My favorite celebrity to impersonate is Peter Falk. My mother and I watch his TV series *Columbo* religiously. Early in season one of its thirteen-year run, I remember trying to imitate Falk's masterful, yet seemingly bumbling detective. During a commercial break, I head to the kitchen to pick up what my mother believes is some kind of treat, but come back instead with a stubby dark pencil in my hand, pretending it's Columbo's ever-present stub of a smoking cigar. I say to my mom, "Ah, excuse me, ma'am, I don't mean to be a pest, it's just that, well, may I say that the pork chops at supper earlier this evening were simply delicious?"

She howls at my impression, and I never look back.

For the next several weeks, I walk around the house as that character until I can think like him . . . which is why I think it's a good—no—a *great* idea to go to the concert dressed as Falk's beloved Lieutenant Columbo.

I'm meticulous in preparing my costume: white shirt, black pants, thin black tie, little cigar stub, and, of course, rumpled beige trench coat borrowed from my best friend Larry Tract's father. (This is why Larry gets to join me at the show. And he feels honored. Which is how he should feel. [Actually, I desperately need a witness and begged him to come with me.])

At first, it seems like a crazy dare to myself, but the more I tell my friends I'm going through with the plan, the more I realize, *Oh shit, I actually have to do this now,* because, now that I've told them, I can't back out at the last second. If I do, I'll never be able to show my face on campus again.

Also, if it goes well, I'm set for life. Connecting with Rich Little on any level will be the first step of my journey to Show Business. I'm not talking about the show business you're thinking of, the show business where movies, television, and famous people come from, but rather the Show Business where dreams are realized and surpassed, where only the greats meet and mingle to share their extraordinary lives.

So no pressure or anything.

Larry and I arrive at the theater minutes before the show begins. As we squeeze into our row and shuffle toward our seats—a couple dozen rows from the stage—I wonder what everyone thinks of my absurd costume. It can't be anything good. I probably come off like that kid dressed as a Klingon at a William Shatner book signing.

My plan for the evening is beautiful in its simplicity: I'm going to wait for the perfect moment in Rich's act, then squeeze out of our row and walk down to the stage as Columbo—slightly hunched over, scratching my head as if lost in thought—then, when I'm within ear-shot of Rich, I'm going to launch into my best Falk voice: "Ahhh, ex-schooshe me, sir, I don't mean to be a pesssht, I don't wanna bother ya, I honeshhhtly don't, but could I assshk ya one question?" And then I'll lean in and do my Falk eye trick—a trick that took me months to master, mind you—which consists of crossing my eyes, then wiggling my left eyeball back and forth. When I do it just right, it looks exactly as if I have a glass eye, just like Falk. (Falk has always been open about his glass eye, which gives a pisher like me the go-ahead to get big laughs from his tragic loss.)

After that's all done, Rich is going to say, "That was very good, very funny," and I'll feel like a billion damn dollars. Actually, come to think of it, this was 1974, and nobody thought in terms of billions, so

I'll only feel like a million. Then I'll head back to my seat and accept congratulations from Larry.

If this brilliant plan is going to work, it's crucial that I pick the perfect moment for my assault. As the show progresses, however, it becomes apparent that this could be a problem because Rich's bits are *long*, involving tons of different voices. There are hardly any breaks, and, while I want to interrupt him, I don't want to *interrupt* interrupt him.

Then it happens! Forty minutes in, during a huge ovation after a six-minute set piece, I realize there isn't going to be a more perfect moment than this.

> As an aside, I should note that, if anyone ever did something like this to me, I would make light of it during the show and then, the moment I got offstage, find out how the fuck the freak was allowed to get anywhere near me.

I'm pumped and fearless, and I'm going to do this no matter what. Nothing is going to stop me from interrupting Rich and the crowd's respective evenings. Nothing in the world.

Except for the goddamn belt on the goddamn trench coat.

As I bolt up out of my seat, ready to charge the stage for my moment of glory in front of my hero, the belt catches in the crack between my and Larry's seats. During the three seconds I'm stuck there, the universe says to me, *Kevin, this is a sign. It is a sign that this may not be a good idea. Sit back down, watch the show, then go home and work on your act so that one day, you'll perform on Carson.*

I tell the universe to go fuck itself, yank off the belt, stumble out of our row, and hustle down front.

Rich has his back to me, and by the time he turns around I'm at the foot of the stage. As the applause dies down, I *am* Peter Falk: "Ahhh, ex-schooshe me sir," I say as loudly as I can without ruining the impression, "I don't mean to be a pesssht . . ." and so on.

The folks seated by the stage, bless their hearts, start chuckling, and the rest of the crowd soon follows suit. Rich does a double take and says, "Oh my goodness! Look who's here! It's Lieutenant Columbo!" The audience's chuckling turns into laughter, and then applause for this absurd moment created by a seventeen-year-old nutcase.

My plan has come to fruition: I'm acknowledged by my hero, and the audience hasn't turned on me, so I'm ready to enjoy the rest of the show. As I turn to head back to my seat, Rich strolls over and says, "So what can I do for you, lieutenant?"

Then he puts the microphone in my face. I'm not ready for that. That isn't part of the plan. He's supposed to say, "Good job, kid," then get back to his performance and then after the show we'd discuss my future.

But I never met a microphone I didn't like, so I keep talking, never breaking character, because I sure as *hell* am not ready to talk to him as Kevin Pollak. If he had said, "That's a very good impression, young man. Tell me about yourself," I would've answered as Peter Falk, and it would've gotten really weird, really fast, as I, natural-born ham or not, would've been that instantly out of my element.

So I say, "I'm shhhhorry to bother ya because I see ya very busy there, what with ya show and all—"

More laughs. *Big* laughs.

He pulls the mic back and dives into his own Columbo impression. One small snag: Columbo isn't part of Rich's roster of celebrity voices. He hasn't, in fact, ever done it on any stage. Within eight seconds, I can tell by the nervous look in his eye that *he* knows his Columbo is terrible, and he knows that *I* know his Columbo is terrible. To his credit, he searches for it, trying hard to make it happen, but it doesn't get any better. So, I suppose in order to dig himself out of the hole, he says, "I'm sorry, you were saying? . . ." then sticks the mic back into my face.

For a moment, I'm speechless, freaked out that I have the better Columbo. Granted, I've never seen him take a crack at Falk on TV, but

I assumed he had it in his back pocket. I hadn't considered that something like this would happen in a million, no, a billion years.

I'm nervous, so my own Columbo goes up a full octave, and I utter something lame like, "Oh, yeshh, I sheee. Well, I washhh, actually . . . just, um . . ."

Yeah.

It's awful, but it gives him the perfect opportunity to send me back to my seat. However, for who-knows-what reason, he says, "Why don't you come on up here onstage, Columbo, and let's figure this out."

I can't explain it, but I'm not even thrown for a nanosecond. I find the side stage steps, then, next thing I know, I'm en route to shake Rich's hand at center stage in front of 2,500 paid customers. Then I experience something that has never happened before and hasn't happened since: My peripheral vision vanishes, replaced by some kind of tunnel vision. I see Rich but am oblivious to the crowd. I truly don't know what to make of this odd sensation as I stroll toward him. I have to wonder: Why is he the only thing I see? Am I dead, and is Rich Little the white light? I'm not frightened, just focused.

"So what can I do for you, lieutenant?"

Now I'm ready to banter and completely improvise the following: "Like I shhhaid, I'm shhhorry to bother ya like this, sir, but shhhix months ago the missus shhhaw in the newshpaper that ya were coming to town, and we got two tickets, but at the last second, the wife became ill. She was heartbroken she couldn't come to da show. But she told me that if I don't get ya autograph, she's not lettin' me back inta da house. So please, Mr. Little, can ya help me out, here?" I dig a piece of paper and a pen out of the pocket of my trench coat—which I'd put there *possibly* to get his autograph *after* the show wherever or whenever the hell that was going happen. (I hadn't thought that far ahead either.) I just imagined that there'd be a line of people and I would join them and, if necessary, sing some Dave Clark Five songs.

As he takes the pen and paper, he spews out what instantly seems to me like Heckler Comeback Stock Line #17: "This guy better watch out, or I'll do Rin Tin Tin and he'll be the tree."

> For those of you who don't get the outdated reference—and don't feel bad if that's the case, because the reference was outdated when he said that about me that fateful night in 1974—Rin Tin Tin was a movie star German shepherd in the 1920s.

Two thoughts zip through my head:

1. Rin Tin Tin, Rich? Way to date yourself by fifty years.
2. You brought me onstage to make fun of me? You couldn't have done it while I was down on the floor?

As the audience laughs, Rich takes my ballpoint pen and, thinking it's a felt-tip, unscrews it from the middle and tries to sign his autograph with the back of the inner copper-tubed ink container.

"Look at this, ladies and gentleman," he says. "Columbo gave me a broken pen."

This plays beautifully into my hands because Columbo was just the kind of guy who would walk around with a pen in his coat pocket that didn't work. So I improvise: "Oh, my, no . . . Ah, jeez, did I do that? I feel harrrrible, just harrrrrible."

"I'll tell you what, lieutenant," he says. "Why don't you get a pen that works, meet me after the show, and I'll sign an autograph for your wife. Ladies and gentlemen, how 'bout a nice round of applause for Lieutenant Columbo!"

A Few Good Words from Kevin's Mom

I couldn't believe it. How could he do that? I was bewildered, just bewildered.

The crowd explodes with applause, and I take my bow. As I jump offstage and float back to my seat, strangers pat me on the back and say, "Great job, great job," and I felt like *$2* billion.

Mr. Little—as I referred to him for the next seven weeks—goes back to work as if nothing ever happened. He does another half an hour, but I barely hear it because the entire time I'm thinking, *When I go backstage, Rich Little is going to take me to Show Business. We're going to get on his private plane, and we'll fly to Show Business, me and Rich. So long, San Jose, California! I'm going to Show Business now.*

At one point, I lean over and whisper to Larry, "You heard him. He asked me to come backstage."

"He sure did, Kevin."

"Me! Backstage!"

"It was amazing."

"I'm going to Show Business."

"You sure are."

"Tell my mom I love her."

"I will, for sure."

"And everybody at school, tell them I love them, too."

"You got it." He pauses, then says, "It kinda stinks that he didn't ask you your name."

"Are you crazy? That would've been horrible."

As the show winds down, I morph into Rich Little's biggest fan on the planet. He can do no wrong. I howl at his Richard Nixon bit and his Sammy Davis Jr. bit and his *other* Richard Nixon bit and his other *other* Nixon bit. But I don't care how many Nixon bits he has because Rich Little is taking me to Show Business, and he's a god. The circular dais is no longer a stage—it's Mount Olympus. And I had stood on the Mountain. Next to Zeus.

It was the greatest single moment of my life.

After Mr. Little says his goodnights, I strut to the backstage area, accepting more congratulations from my fellow audience members along the way. Their praise is all fine and good, but it slows me down, so by the time I'm backstage, there's a line of thirty people waiting to get an autograph from the great Rich Little.

At that moment, I have three choices:

1. Walk up to my new pal Mr. Little and announce that I'm ready for our trip to Show Business.

2. Nicely ask to take cuts near the front of the line, comfortable in the thought that everybody else will recognize me and comply . . . if not insist that letting me go first is the right thing to do.

3. Be polite, and go to the back of the line.

Yep, #3.

It still strikes me as inexplicable that the nervy kid who dressed up as a famous television detective and interrupted Little's act in front of a sold-out house—only to be asked by the master to join him onstage *and* to join him backstage after the show, not to mention who thoroughly deluded himself into thinking that he was about to board a private jet, destination Show Business—would *choose* at that moment to be like everybody else and politely get in line.

Almost immediately, another dozen or so people line up behind me, and I feel sad for them. After all, when I get up there, Rich and I are going to Show Business, so they aren't going to get an autograph. I'm going to get a seat on the private plane, and they'll get nothing. I don't want to tell them that, of course. Surely Mr. Little will know how best to deliver this sort of disappointing news.

As I get closer to Rich, I hear what he's saying to his fans as he signs his name on their ticket stubs, programs, or hands: "Hi! What's your name? Debbie? Thank you for coming, Debbie." Then he autographs and returns the item, then immediately turns to the next person in line: "Hi! What's your name? Steve? Thanks for coming to the show, Steve." Then the next person in line: "Hi! What's your name? Jimmy? Nice to see you. Thanks for coming."

And so on. (I was making note of this, in preparation for my not-too-distant future Show Business duties.)

Then it's my turn.

When Rich sees it's me, his face lights up like a Hanukkah bush. In a hale, hearty tone—a tone three billion times haler and heartier than he'd used with anybody else—he said, "Hey, there he is! What's your name?"

"Kevin."

"Kevin! That was very good, Kevin." Then he signs an autograph with a "Thanks for coming" and looks over my shoulder at the average citizen behind me, and says, "Hi! What's your name?"

It was astounding that he'd brought me up onstage, but this is far and away more shocking. Sure, in the decades that follow, I will come to understand that anticipation is the root of all disappointment, but . . . *not now!* This is *wildly* uncharted territory of heartbreak. I was *way* more crushed than I would ever be getting dumped by a girl. I'm near tears, but how can I not be? This is the man who was supposed to take me to Show Business, but instead he'd shuffled me off to motherfucking Buffalo? (No offense, Buffaloians, if "Buffaloians" is a thing, but even *you* have to appreciate its use here.)

Utterly devastated and in a fog, I step to the side and think, *Should I wait here for him? Am I getting on that private plane after he finishes signing the rest? No. I can't stay. He treated me the same as he treated everybody who* wasn't *onstage with him. I got the message. Message received.*

Then I go home. Show Business will have to wait.

Postscript

Many years later, I caught up with Rich at The Tonight Show *and reminded him of the night we shared the revolving stage. I thanked him again for bringing me up and confessed my foolish post-show dreams of riding the heavens with him to Show Business. When I asked why the Buffalo shuffle, he confessed that he was fearful of what kind of weirdo would do what I did and what he might do in the future. Alas, I could understand and actually appreciate that explanation.*

Post-Postscript

For the next ten years, whenever I went to a gig, I carted only a single prop to the music halls and comedy clubs up and down the San Francisco peninsula. That prop? Larry's father's jacket. It was the cherry on my Columbo sundae.

Needless to say, I ditched the fucking belt.

3

Tripping Past Dad

For thirty years, my father worked for Sears as a kitchen designer and salesman. Back in his day, the salesmen didn't only stand on the show-room floor among the washers, dryers, and refrigerators, waiting for a shopper to stroll by like they do today (or like my character did in *Avalon*). They met potential buyers on the floor and showed them their latest wares, but then they made an appointment to drive out to their home and measure their kitchen space. Then they went to their drafts-man tables and hand-drew, free style, what always looked to me like The Kitchen of Tomorrow, replete with gleaming floors and sparkling, newfangled hardware.

My father did all this on spec, mind you, in hopes of selling his customers some Sears kitchen appliances. Consequently, he was at his drafting board each night until two in the morning. Naturally, I was proud of my pops and often marveled at his drawings and also how the artistic aspect of his work stood out as an anomaly in his otherwise artistic-free existence. But when I was a teenager, getting past him at the drafting table at night when I was drunk or stoned was impossible.

Each and every night, he's at his worktable, just off the kitchen. If I come home high and go through the front door and directly to my room, he doesn't see me and I'm fine. The later I get home, though, the more likely he is to call me into the kitchen with a "How was your night?" which means I can't just yell, "Fine, I'm going to bed!" and hide in safety.

Mind you, he's not staying up late because he's worried. No, my dad's hard at work, and also OK with me getting in after 11:00 on a school night, but after midnight he wants a look-see, which means on one particularly late summer night out I had to go and shoot the shit.

Generally, I related the acceptable parts of the evening's festivities—"We just drove around in Chuck's car most of the night. We stopped for Breakfast Jack's, but nothing to really report." That usually did it. On the night in question, however, I don't get home until after 1:00 a.m. and then try to sneak past him.

While high on 'shrooms.

For the first time.

He calls me in, and, before I say a single word, he stands up from his drafting table and says, "We need to have a talk."

Dad hadn't ever said those words in that order, and, psilocybin mushrooms or not, this is a tad more than your typical *Dad isn't happy* or even *Dad is really pissed*. This is something else altogether.

Did I mention that this is my first time on 'shrooms?

He leads me out to the porch and sits me down. "Have I done a good job of raising you and your brother?"

I can't answer right away, for many reasons, the least of which is that now he resembles Father Christmas, with the flowing white beard. *Whoa.*

Then he pours out his heart. "I hope I've done right by you and Craig. I tried my hardest to make sure you both knew right from wrong, but sometimes I just don't know if I succeeded. Do you think I have?"

Again, I can't answer because now he's a farmer wearing a giant straw hat and has a long, thin stalk of wheat in his mouth . . . Holy shit, that's a pitchfork in his fucking hand! As I gawk at the pitchfork, he tells me, "You and your brother growing up were little demons," and he turns into Satan, with horns and a crazy, deep, scary laugh: *Bwhuh huh huh huh huhhhhhhhh!!!* And then in quick succession he morphs into a grandfather clock, my mother, and Rascal, our cat.

I stare at my shoes because I don't want to see what he'll turn into next. "I don't mean to be disrespectful, Dad, and I *do* think you've done a great job as a father, but I don't feel well, and I should go to sleep. Can we get into this tomorrow, please?"

He dismisses me, thankfully, and I head straight to bed, where I dream of living on Main Street at Disneyland as a good little boy who doesn't smoke pot or eat mushrooms that taste like dirty socks and turn his dad into John Carpenter's *The Thing*.

4

Learning to Stand Up

By the time I reach Pioneer High School—Mustangs forever!—I'm a professional stand-up comedian. Granted, my only paying gig was at my junior high school vice principal's Elks Club, but it earned me a sawbuck. Thus, I'm a pro.

Most importantly, I've moved beyond lip-synching—some might even say I'm developing an act—and am experimenting with impressions beyond Columbo, most notably our school's football coach. He's an easy target: He has a weird, staccato voice; when he lumbers across the school, his head wobbles from side to side.

One afternoon, I'm hanging out in the quad, entertaining my pals with the football coach impression. Right when I'm about to launch into the finale, I find myself in a headlock—the kind that, within six seconds, you know you're about to pass out. Right before I drift off into dreamland, the very coach in question whispers into my ear, "Just so you know, I don't think it's funny."

When the coach lets me go, I rub my neck, thinking, *Y'know, I could probably impersonate Marlon Brando, and chances are fairly good that he'd never find out and/or get me into a headlock.*

After that realization, I work on the impressions of the day—most notably Brando, specifically from *The Godfather,* and President Nixon—which I perform for my fellow stoners while hanging out in local parks after school dances. What sort of stage could I use for these shows, you ask? Why, the tops of picnic benches, of course. I've cobbled together enough of an act that, after the most popular girl in school catches it, she suggests setting up an audition for me in front of her boyfriend, who happens to front the biggest live musical act in town, the Joe Sharino Band.

Then, as now, Joe leads one of the most crowd-pleasing cover bands in the South Bay, and at that point in my young actually-talking-and-not-lip-synching stand-up career it's just as likely as being asked to audition for the Beatles. But, still smarting from my encounter with Rich Little, I don't expect Joe to put me on his private jet and take me to Show Business.

I call Joe, and he tells me, "Come to the house tomorrow after school. I'll see your act, and we'll see if you're any good."

I'm impressed by the "come to my house" part because I don't know anyone who owns a house other than my parents and my friends' parents, so I expect to be impressed.

I'm not.

His living room, where I audition, is smallish and insignificant. I figured a guy who makes girls swoon the way Joe does would have a living room that looked a little swanky, but, once I factor in that it's the first single guy's house that I've seen, I return my focus to impressing him, which leads me to my next concern.

This room is not conducive for comedy.

To this point, aside from my gig on the Zuckers' fireplace, I've performed for relatively large audiences, but at Joe's house the audience was Joe. Over the years, I've performed for countless private and corporate functions, where the rule of thumb is: The bigger the payday, the worse the crowd. The other rule of thumb is: The smaller the crowd, the harder and quicker the laughter dies, and thus the harder the gig. Even the best of us has burned through ninety minutes of material in forty-five minutes when facing a small crowd. And here I am performing the most important set of my career up until then, and it's for a party of one.

After the first sentence of my act, the air completely sucks out of the room. I finish the bit, and Joe smiles brightly. "Good. Good." No laughter. I do another bit, Joe smiles brightly. "Nice. Nice." Still no laughter.

It's painful. *So* painful. I've bombed many times since, but I've never felt as alone as I did standing in front of Joe Sharino's couch, which I joke to myself looks like something right from *The Mary Tyler Moore Show* collection in order to forget my present agony.

On stage at the Comedy Day Celebration in Golden Gate Park in San Francisco in front of forty thousand people. This annual free show, which features about eighty comedians, is proof positive that San Francisco has always been one of the most supportive stand-up cities in the country.

After I finish, he stands up. "I'm doing The Garrett in Campbell on Friday. I take three ten-minute breaks. Can you fill them all?"

That was the beginning of my career as a set-break comedian. There are dozens of bars in the area that book musicians to play on their tiny stages off in the corner, and, once I start performing regularly at these shitty, loud, rude, obnoxious fucking bars, I know without a doubt that this is my future. It's the summer of 1975, I'm seventeen, a recent high school graduate desperately trying to get laughs from drunks, and the happiest person you've ever met.

Postscript

When I enter the San Francisco Comedy Competition for the first of what will be three times in 1978—and I kill in my first set—there's a palpable sense of, Who the fuck is this guy, and why is he so confident?

Here's a tip: Performing three seemingly endless years of stand-up in the little bars around San Jose—where there are no comedy clubs filled with people who actually want to see you—will teach you how to get laughs when nobody's paying attention. If you can get those fuckers to laugh, you can get anybody to.

Post-Postscript

Before one of my early Tonight Show appearances, I get a call from Jay Leno, who will be subbing for Johnny Carson the night I'm on. Jay, quite the mentor to us up-and-coming comedians, says, "You wanna come up to the house and run the material you're doing on the show?"

I say yes, go up to the house, run the material, and . . . it's _worse_ than Sharino.

Joe was a musician, and he was at least smiling because there was a comedian in his living room, being funny just for him. Jay, on the other hand, was _the_ comedian, and he wasn't smiling.

After I do the first impression, he looks at me and nods. "So . . . does that normally work in the act?" to which I offer a look of _Are you_ _KIDDING_ me? He quickly says, "It's fine, it's fine! If it normally works, great, great."

The second joke, still no laugher: "And . . . that also normally works?" followed by the same look from me, to which he again spits out, "Good, good, good, good! As long as you've done it and you know it worked." I'm sure he wanted me to do well for my own good, as well as his own understandable needs of doing the best show possible as Johnny's

Guest Host. I can't imagine the sort of pressure he must've been under, but he filled me with so much self-doubt that I thought he truly hated everything I did.

After my segment on the show is done and Jay throws it to commercial, he leans over and says, "You know, Rich Little is getting on in age, and there's nobody in your generation who's the impressionist. I know you've said you wanna do this acting thing, and you came on the show as an actor, not a comedian, but you should really think about it because, if you wanted to, you could be the impressionist. You have that level of talent. I'm serious, you could take over."

To reiterate: If you're just starting out and have the chance to perform stand-up comedy in front of drunks in a bar, do it. Work through the pain, and stand tall. If you survive, it'll only get easier.

To make sure it only gets easier, never perform in front of just one person, regardless of whether that person is parked on an expensive Italian, handmade leather chair or Lou Grant's sofa.

5

John Belushi Takes a Knee

Having started my stand-up comedy career in San Francisco, I become close with the legendary then-Bay-Area-based concert promoter Bill Graham. One of his venues is the Old Waldorf, where he's hired me to open for acts like Pat Benatar, during her debut album tour; Robbie Robertson of The Band; Bette Midler, Barry Manilow's former boss; and many others. Eventually his company opened a comedy club in what used to be the Waldorf's additional-dressing-rooms-and-storage area, which he dubbed The Punchline. The Punchline becomes my home court, and it's always a thrill performing when I know that Bill is in the house.

One night after a show, I meet him at the bar, where he says, "I'm just coming from seeing this new act at one of my clubs, and, Kevin, I'm telling you, this kid is going to be the biggest thing in music, and I've seen them all. His show took my breath away. It was like the Second Coming."

Bill was one of the most important figures in rock history—he founded the Fillmore clubs, he was road manager for the Rolling Stones, and on, and on—so when he says somebody took his breath away, you pull up a chair and listen.

"This act was like a bizarre combination of Jimi Hendrix and James Brown. He plays an amazing guitar, and he dances and sings like a motherfucker. He's mind-bogglingly original."

"This sounds like the greatest act that ever lived," I say. "What's his name?"

"Well," Bill sighs, "that's the problem. His name is Prince."

"What do you mean? Prince of where?"

"No, that's it. He calls himself 'Prince.'"

"Not, 'Prince' something?"

"Just 'Prince.'"

"'*Prince*'?"

"'*Prince*'!"

"Well, he may've blown you away tonight, but that name is ridiculous," I say.

"It's OK," Bill says, "because this guy is gonna take over the world."

Like I said, Bill was a genius who knew a genius when he saw or heard one. Me? I just thought his name was bullshit. Of course, in retrospect, it's not that awful. Not like The Artist Formerly Known As Prince or just using a symbol as a name—'cause that *is* bullshit.

I often collide with the music world and even go on a brief tour with singer/songwriter Dave Mason. (Dave, who used to be in the band Traffic, cut a version of "All Along the Watchtower" that is spectacular.) At one point in our little run, we have a couple shows at the Old Waldorf, a stage on which I'm quite comfortable. The backstage area at the Waldorf is a great rock 'n' roll hang, replete with pool table and all kinds of little rooms where people do . . . stuff. What stuff? Never you mind, as my grandfather used to say.

One evening, I roll in for work at the Old Waldorf, and there at the pool table, cues in hand, are John Belushi and Van Morrison.

My heart stops.

Mason's leaning against the wall, laughing his ass off about something, so I'm not sure he even notices me. Morrison, of course, is rock 'n' roll royalty of a level beyond Mount Rushmore, but to me—the stand-up comedian—John Belushi is the new King of Comedy, and I can't tear my eyes away. This is 1979, and he's riding as high off *Saturday Night Live* as anyone ever would in the history of the show. He's also stolen the hearts and souls of comedy fans with his work in *Animal House*, which had hit theaters only a few months before. Needless to say, he's much more of a hero to me than Van Morrison.

I don't want to bother anybody, so I give Mason a wave, then become a proverbial fly on the wall. Belushi's presence is so immense that it all but freezes me, though, like I've never been since. He's not doing anything funny, but just being who he is, which, at twenty-two years old, has my head spinning. I mean, I'm in the presence of a greatness more powerful than anything I'd ever experienced. I watch him for a good long time, and eventually Van has to be elsewhere and says his goodbyes. Before I can say a word to Dave or Sir John, the two of them wander off into one of these dressing rooms that surround the pool table area and close the door behind them.

Soon, the smell of smoke seeps from under the door of said dressing room, and, even though I don't smoke, I decide I have to get into that room. I hatch a plan: I'll walk in and say something, *anything*, to Dave, and he'll feel obligated to introduce me to John, who in turn could say absolutely nothing. Honestly, it didn't matter. I just wanted to soak up some more of his presence.

I work up the courage to knock on the door. After a second, somebody mumbles "Come in." I enter, close the door behind me, and take in the scene: Belushi is leaning against a wall, Mason is on the floor, and the room is filled with so much smoke that I can barely see. It's like a steam room, thick with a gaseous cloud that makes you forget why you came in. Belushi passes a joint to Mason, who takes a toke—what? That's what we called it in 1979—sees me, and laugh-chokes because he's come up with what he believes to be a brilliant idea.

"Columbo!" he says, pointing to me. He's seen my impression a dozen times. Then he points to the joint and, smiling like the village idiot, repeats, "Columbo!"

I try to match his enthusiastic smile, but all I can think is, *Yeah, Dave, I get it. You're smoking Columbian Gold, which you're calling "Columbo." It's hysterical. If I were stoned, I'd probably be laughing, too, but I'm not, so fucking introduce me to Belushi, already, will ya?!*

Refusing to waste this opportunity just because Dave's too high to make introductions, I take this invitation to get into Belushi's face and launch into my Peter Falk impression. I get the one eye moving, gesturing as if I have a stubby cigar in my hand, while saying, "Ahhhh, exschooose me, sir. Is that . . . *marijuana?*"

Belushi busts out laughing, and I'm floating a few inches off the ground. I don't let him breathe, though: "I'm shorry to be a pest, but I'm gonna hafta confiscate whatever you have on you. Ya know, for the fellas down at the precinct. I'm happy with just the cigah heah, but they can put that stuff away like nobody's business. Anyway, if ya wouldn't mind too much, just put what you have in my pockets, please."

Much to my delight, Belushi bends over, bobs his head, and laughs his ass off. Then, still cracking up and leaning against the wall, he slowly sinks down into a crouching position with his arms on top of his thighs.

My Columbo impression literally brought John Belushi to his knees. Upon realizing this, my heart froze for the second time that night.

Still one of the top five moments of my life.

6

Larry, It's Albert/It's Kevin/It's Albert

Well before he was on CNN, Larry King had an overnight syndicated show on Mutual Radio that ran five nights a week from midnight to 3:00 a.m. Larry was a great broadcaster even back then, and I was in the habit of listening to him on the way home from gigs, so it was a thrill when one night a friend named Rich Lieberman tells me, "I've got the hotline number to Larry's show. You should call into the show as Albert Brooks." Albert was one of Larry's regular call-in guests, and Rich knew that I had developed a pretty strong Brooks impersonation.

I am obsessed with the comedic mind of Albert Brooks—I can still recite *Modern Romance* practically from beginning to end—so I tell Rich, "Oh man, that would be amazing."

Minutes later, I make the call. Larry picks up, and I hear That Voice say, "We go to San Francisco, hello."

In my best Albert Brooks: "Larry? Larry, it's Albert. How are ya, buddy? Listen, I'm calling from San Francisco because I'm here visiting a girl and . . . well, that's not important. What *is* important, is that I'm listening to the show, and I wanted to see how you're doing. We haven't talked in awhile."

Larry says, "Let me go on record as saying that while I do not believe this is the *real* Albert Brooks, that's the best Albert Brooks impression I have ever heard. Who *is* this?"

"I'm sorry, Larry," I say, breaking character. "My friend put me up to this. My name is Kevin Pollak. I'm a stand-up comedian out of San Francisco, and I listen to you every night, so I know that Albert calls in, and—"

"Listen to me, Kevin Pollak. *You* are gonna be a *star*. Do you do other impressions?" I give him some Columbo and some Carson. *"You're a great talent, young man. I look forward to seeing much more*

Let's go to the phones. Rantoul, Illinois, you're on with Kevin Pollak.

of you in the very near future. That's Kevin Pollak, ladies and gentlemen. Look for him, a rising young comedian. And we'll be back after these messages. Wow . . ."

I can hear that wow just before the commercial began, and I'm beyond excited, deciding in that moment of pure joy that I'll be calling in soon and often. The King had knighted me, and I'm going to lean way into this new opportunity.

Not too long after, Larry has me on the show in his D.C. studio. He tells his audience of our first conversation, demands that I do my Brooks, then asks me to explain to his listeners how I honed the impression.

"For a long time, the outgoing message on my answering machine was me doing my Albert Brooks impression. When it still needed work, my friends would leave a message saying, 'Hi, Kevin, it's Steve. That's a terrible Albert Brooks. Call me back,' I'd know it needed work.

Eventually, I got a message along the lines of, 'Hi, Kevin, it's Rick. Don't forget we're playing poker Thursday night. And that's a great Albert Brooks. I was hoping you'd get better at doing him,' *then* I knew it was ready.

"But one day, I'm at home writing, and the phone rings. I let the machine pick it up, and I hear, 'Hi, Kevin, you don't know me, but this is Rob Reiner.' I freeze where I'm standing. Rob continues, 'I grew up with Albert Brooks. He's one of my best friends, and that's an unbelievable impression of him. What's really amazing is that's not how he sounds when he's performing onstage or acting in a movie. That's how he sounds around the house.' He laughs, then says, 'Just wanted to tell you that. OK, bye.'

"This call sends me dancing around my little apartment in sheer jubilation for about forty-five seconds. That's how long it takes me to realize that not only did I not know Rob, I hadn't met *any* filmmakers yet. I thought, *I just had a chance to talk to Rob Reiner, and I didn't. Why would I not talk to him? Why would I not allow him to compliment the hell out of me and ask me more questions about impersonations? Then maybe he'd come and see me perform somewhere, and he'd audition me for a film . . . IDIOT!!* Oh, but there's more.

"Over the next ninety minutes, my phone rings twenty times— back then there was no caller ID, so you had to screen every call— and each time after the outgoing message played, the caller hung up. Finally, somebody said something: 'Hi, this is Carl Reiner . . .' By now, I'm ready to talk to *any* Reiner, so I dive to the phone and say hello to Rob's brilliant dad. Carl says, 'Hi, Kevin. Listen, I heard about your Albert Brooks impression from my business partner, George Shapiro. George is Jerry Seinfeld's manager, and Jerry told us both about your outgoing message, so I had to call. This is not the first time I've called, by the way . . . I don't know if you know this, but that impression of yours is all over town now.'

"I tell Carl that I'd had about twenty hang-ups, then he says, 'Well, I don't imagine that many people would leave a message.'

"I told him, 'Your son left a message.'"

"He said, 'Yes, I'm the one who told him about it. Also, so you know, Rob called Albert, and then apparently Albert called you but didn't leave a message. Then he called Rob right back and said, 'Really, Rob? Is that what you think I sound like? It sounds like my Uncle *Zeke*.'"

Here's where my first visit to Larry's radio show takes a historic turn. After I finish telling Larry and his listeners the story, Albert Brooks calls into the show and says, "Hi, Larry. It's Albert. I'm in the car. What the hell is going on here?"

"Oh my God, ladies and gentlemen," Larry said, "you've been listening to Kevin Pollak doing Albert Brooks, and we've been talking about our great mutual love and appreciation for Albert, and now we've got the *real* Albert on the phone. Albert, what do you think? The kid's pretty good, isn't he?"

"Listen, Larry," Albert said, "let me tell you that, when I first heard Kevin do the impression on the show, I called my attorney—he has an 800 number—and I asked him if there was anything legally inappropriate about this. He said there wasn't, and I said, 'Well then it's a *good thing*.'"

"What do you think of Kevin's story about doing you on his answering machine?" Larry asks.

"Yes, I did call your answering machine, Kevin, that story *is* true, but the impression sounds much better now. What kind of answering machine is that?"

There I am, listening to my hero riff on the radio, dying with excitement, and laughing uncontrollably at his improvs—"What kind of machine is that?"

"I had a problem earlier, Larry," Albert continues. "I was listening to the show and Kevin's story, and a cop pulls me over. I told him, 'They're doing me on the radio, officer,' so he started listening to the show, and he hears Kevin, he hears me, and then he gave me *two* tickets."

Fast-forward a few months. I'm crawling into bed early one night when I get a call from a friend named Jimmy Miller. Dennis Miller's brother, Jimmy, is one of the most powerful managers in show business. He represents Will Ferrell and Judd Apatow among others. Back when I was hanging out with him, he was booking The Comedy & Magic Club in Hermosa Beach.

But Enough about You . . . Dennis Miller
I'm convinced that Pol-man's William Shatner impression actually revealed to Shatner just how he should do Shatner to make a fortune doing Shatner.

"Albert just walked into the Improv," Jimmy says, "Get down here."

He, too, knows of my devotion to Master Brooks.

> In fact, do me and yourself a favor: Take a twenty-minute break from reading this book, go directly to YouTube, and spend some time with young Albert Brooks to see why this man's skills helped shape what funny was for a generation. His birth name was Albert Einstein. Just sayin'.

I lived about eight blocks from the famed comedy club on Melrose Avenue—known as the Melrose Improv then, and the Hollywood Improv now—so I'm there immediately. Off in the corner of the club, there's Albert, kibitzing with the Improv's owner, Budd Friedman, among others, all of whom are sitting at Budd's Table. Few comedians dared to sit at Budd's Table because, well, it was Budd's Table. But somebody of Albert's stature was more than welcome to hold court.

Albert, in the middle of telling everybody at the full table a story about his father, glances at me and senses how desperate I am to sit at the table. Thing is, there aren't any empty seats. So off he goes:

"I don't know if you guys realize this, but my father was a radio comic"—without looking up—"Hey, Kevin, why don't you grab a seat? So, my dad was a radio comic back in the thirties, named Park Your Carcass."—still hasn't looked my way—"Kevin, you're making me nervous, sit down. See, my father is buried at one of these celebrity cemeteries areas."—He looks up at me ever-so quickly.—"Kevin, really, sit. And buried next to dad is Shemp Howard from the Three Stooges, and I have this recurring nightmare . . ."—waving his hands at me—"Seriously, Kev, pick a chair! I have this nightmare that I'm at my father's grave, and I'm paying my respects very sincerely and somberly, and I look over, and there's Moe Howard, kneeling at Shemp's grave, and he's stabbing at the dirt in front of the headstone with *two fingers*, and he's saying, 'You bastard, I can't get work as a single!'"

While everybody laughs hysterically, Albert looks at me, smiles, and says, 'So, you're not gonna sit?'"

A bit later, Albert takes the stage. I've never seen anybody of that stature perform at the Improv; for that matter, I've never seen a true hero perform in that small a venue. (I'd seen Steve Martin do stand-up ten years prior at a casino in Lake Tahoe for maybe 600 people. The Improv holds, at best, 105 . . . until the fire marshal stops by, at which point it drops to 89.) More importantly, I've never seen anybody do what he does, which is completely improvising a forty-five-minute stand-up act. His subject matter is very near and dear: Why Sean Connery is going to win an Oscar and I'm not. (This is 1987, and Albert and Sean are both up for Best Supporting Actor, Albert for *Broadcast News* and Sean for *The Untouchables*.)

It's a stand-up comedy clinic—at once personal and stream-of-consciousness—the greatest stand-up set I would ever see, bar none. After his set, he walked past me as I sat at a table with others—we were still applauding—and said, "Oh, how nice, you found a seat."

I laughed from my comfy chair. "That was a stand-up comedy clinic, truly."

To which he replied: "Thanks. Would mean so much more if you were standing now. How ironic."

7

Torturing Reiser, Part One

As I work my way up the stand-up comedy food chain in San Francisco, I meet a lot of the performers who, at that point, are making it in Los Angeles. As much as we were trained in S.F. to hate the sell-outs from L.A., they couldn't be nicer; Jerry Seinfeld, for instance, offers to show me around the city "when you finally come, and you will." But I'm especially keen to meet a guy named Paul Reiser, whom I've seen perform a hilarious and intelligent act on *The Tonight Show*.

My interest in meeting Paul peaks when I see him in the Barry Levinson film *Diner*. I walk out of the theater, thinking, clear as a bell, *There's a comic who's doing what I want to do. His stand-up is strong enough to get on The Tonight Show, and here he is, acting in a film that isn't just a jokey-jokey, silly comedy, or even a smart, funny one, but rather a film with nuanced and dramatic characters, conversations, and stories.*

When I hear that Paul is doing stand-up at Cobb's in San Francisco, I devise the perfect way to ingratiate myself: I'm going to call the guy who runs Cobb's—whose name is, believe it or not, Tom Sawyer—find out what hotel Reiser's staying at, and ring him up . . . as Peter Falk.

"Paaaaaul? Is thish Paaaaaul Reis-uh?"

"I'm sorry, but do I know you?"

"It's Peter Falk. Listen, I'm in town, I saw ya name on the marquee over at, what is it . . . aw, jeez . . . Cobb's, I think, and, uh, I'm heah with some friends, and we'd like to come to the show."

Reiser buys it instantly. "Oh. My goodness. Mr. Falk. Hello. How many people in your party? What show do you want to come to? I am so tickled. You don't understand, sir, you've been a hero of mine for a very long time. My friends and I, we watch your films all the time and *Columbo,* too. I am so tickled. I'm a big fan of your early work. *Murder,*

Incorporated, for example. When I tell my mother and father that you called, they'll be *so* tickled, really."

Paul's so sweet and wonderful that I instantly feel horrible. I mean, look, I feel *terrific* about the immediate validation he gives me for my impression, but the thing is, now I can't stop doing Falk. Paul's been so genuine and, quite frankly, vulnerable, that if I stop and introduce myself he'll never, ever talk to me again. More likely, he'll curse my name for the rest of our lives.

So I tell him, as Falk, that something has just come up, and I quickly hang up.

For the next thirty minutes, I stare at the wall, thinking, *Fuck. Now what?* I finally realize the right thing to do—the only thing to do—is to suck it up, call him back, and explain why I did this horrible thing to someone whom I admire so very much. The question is, do I call him back as Falk, then break character and introduce myself, or do I call him back as me, confess my sins, and then tell him what a big fan I am and beg his forgiveness, but add that if he can't forgive me I'll certainly understand because I'm not convinced I could forgive anyone who'd done that to me—?

I go with plan B.

"Hi, Paul, my name is Kevin Pollak. I'm a local comedian, and I'm a huge fan, and you're a total inspiration to me because all I want to do is act in movies. I know you're pals with Jerry Seinfeld, and I opened up for him a couple of months ago, and I'm looking forward to coming out to see your show tomorrow night."

"Thank you very much. I'll call Jerry in a couple of minutes and check out your story to see if you are who you say you are."

We share our first laugh, and I feel a nanosecond of relief, which, another nanosecond later, evaporates.

"Great, and by the way, I'm unbelievably sorry to tell you that I called you as Peter Falk half an hour ago. That was not Falk. That was me."

A loooooong pause.

"Are you serious?" Reiser asks quietly.

This reminds me of two things: 1) I actually wore a tie onstage to perform in an otherwise casual comedy club—in this case the *great* Comedy Works in Denver (love you, Wendy and gang)—and B) I had a lot of hair in my twenties.

"Yeah."

Another looooooong pause.

"Do it again. Let me hear it." After two sentences of Falk, he interrupts with "You son of a bitch. Oh, Jesus. Oh, my God. Well, that's a heartbreaker for me, isn't it?"

"Paul, I'm *so* sorry that I couldn't stop right away and tell you, but it's only because you were being so sweet and you were so enam—"

"Yeah, you really let me go there, didn't you? Wasn't enough for you to get a couple of laughs. You had to go on for, what, ten minutes, was it? You're not a nice person. That's clear to me now."

Later that week, we shared a meal together, the first of countless others, and we've remained friends ever since.

That is until I left a message on his answering machine as Alan Arkin . . .

8

The King and I

Taking the reins of your career—especially if you're trying to wedge your way into Show Business—can be scary. Or suicidal. One wrong decision can send you into the toilet, and you'll be forced to sign on for a six-month residency at Ira's Giggle Igloo in Frostbitten Balls, Wisconsin. Or, horror of horrors, you might have to live by your convictions, and *that*, my friend is a lonely place to be.

But sometimes, no matter how frightening, you have to seize control of your destiny because nobody else is going to care about you or your career the way you do, whether your career is making people laugh or making people wedding cakes. You're the one on the front lines each and every day, so you have a pretty damn good idea how the world feels about you and your work. Sure, you might have a wonderful agent, manager, or sales rep, but you're always going to be your best advocate because you care about you more than anybody, and you know you better than anybody. Not to mention that those *wonderful* agents and managers have a ton of other clients, and you have just the one: you. Sometimes that means making hard decisions without the benefit of a second pair of eyes, ears, or balls, but on a certain level it's better that you suffer from your own mistakes than somebody else's. It's easier to point the finger at somebody else, yeah, but it's healthier to point it at yourself. The spoils go to the victor, but you rarely learn shit from success. So-called failure, on the other hand, is brimming with truly useful lessons.

Deep down, I always knew all of this, even though not a single person in my life bothered to mention it. It was yet another hugely important lesson I had to learn on my own—which isn't a bad thing because figuring shit out for yourself makes it more substantial and lasting. When did I learn this lesson? When I finally got my shot to be on *The Tonight Show*.

Performing stand-up on *The Tonight Show* had been a dream since childhood. I grew up mentally collecting comedians the way other kids physically collected baseball cards. Back in the late-sixties, we had a choice between Bill Cosby, Bob Newhart, Jonathan Winters, Alan King, Lenny Bruce, Don Rickles, Henny Youngman, Phyllis Diller, Shelley Berman, and *maybe* a dozen others, all of whom, by the time they were in our living rooms, were polished performers. What mesmerized me the most were their comings and goings on *Carson.* That was where the magic happened, and I report that fact with 100 percent certainty because, from the age of ten on, I rarely miss an episode.

My mom and dad are not cool with me watching each and every night—most parents don't want their preteen staying up until 1:00 in the morning—and it becomes a *thing.* But my parents are no fools, and they start using my obsession as a bargaining chip. *Mow the lawn, and you can watch Johnny. Clean your room, and you can watch Johnny. Eat the vegetables that I've boiled until they have no flavor, nutrients, or color, and you can watch Johnny.*

As I race into my adolescence, I notice a trend on the show: the bigger and/or better comedians are no longer doing straight stand-up routines. Johnny introduces them, and they head directly over to King Carson's throne for an interview. Guys like Albert Brooks, Rodney Dangerfield, Steve Martin, and Don Rickles were Couch Comedians. They still do their act, but it's in the guise of a conversation from that couch, that prized perch for movie stars from yesterday and today or the odd six-year-old kid who could outsmart everyone. Carson always displays an ability to converse with all ages, but more importantly he's a great listener.

As I watch the evolution of stand-up to sit-down, I figure out that being a Couch Comedian who appears in the first segment is far more prestigious than being a regular comic who does his six minutes at the end of the show.

A Couch Comedian. *Yeah.*

I'm twenty-eight years old when the final piece of this puzzle finally clicks into place on the board for me: The Couch Comedian is a friend of the King, not just his jester. I'm working regularly alongside many of the big-name comedians who'd appeared on the show. I find out about a thing called "spontaneous paneling." Being spontaneously paneled means that once you finish your six minutes on the star in the center of the stage—which, you Carson-o-philes will be interested to know, lay three feet away from the star on which Carson stood during his mono-logue—Johnny waves you over to the couch for a quick chat.

> This is rare for comics debuting on the show; I think it only happened about a half a dozen times among the comedians of my generation, and when it did happen it was a *huge* fucking deal. Roseanne Barr was spontaneously paneled, as was Drew Carey, both of whom killed, and both of whom deserved the honor. This wasn't just a luck-of-the-draw event. Carson knew great talent the first time he saw it. He wanted to knight the gifted few . . . and maybe he used it as a tool to add to his legend.

I also learn that for a first-timer, there's a set protocol dictated by Johnny's legendary segment producer/talent coordinator/gatekeeper—an eternally sourpussed man named Jim McCauley. The stand-up com-edy appearance protocol is simple: You aren't allowed to look at Johnny until you finish your routine. Even then, you can look at him only once. If Johnny thinks you did well, he'll shoot you a thumb-and-index-finger OK sign. If you get a smile but no OK sign, you aren't coming back anytime soon. If you get the wave from him, you get the fuck over to that couch and you sit the fuck down. In other words, don't stand there pointing at yourself, saying, "Me? What? You want *me*? Gosh, *really*?"

When I arrive in town in the fall of 1983—one year almost to the day after I took second place in the San Francisco International Stand-Up Comedy Competition, officially becoming big in the small pond—there are two comedy clubs in L.A. where McCauley fishes for new talent, The Comedy Store and The Improv. When he's debating whether to bring new blood onto the show, the comics call it circling, as in, "Who's Jim circling tonight?" McCauley's presence in a club spikes our competitiveness—we all want to be the one being sought—but we still all support the circled comic. That said, when we're out in the restaurant area of The Improv, there's some extra angling to get onstage for McCauley.

Jim has worked on *The Tonight Show* forever, and Johnny trusts that he'll hire only the best comedians out there. Still, as powerful as Jim has become, he has palpable concerns of his own. It's said that at one point he booked an act who choked so badly onscreen that Johnny told him, "The next time you bring me a comedian who's not ready, I'll tear off your head and shit down your neck."

McCauley has another reason to be careful: When Johnny really takes to an act, he announces on the show "That was just marvelous, wow. Folks, you'll see him back real soon." Which means that McCauley has to book the comic back in the next week or three, so he has to know for certain that the comic has another tight six minutes in hand. So McCauley won't invite a comic on until he or she has not one but *two* television-ready routines, which is why he's been known to circle for months—if only to cover his own neck.

I'm twenty-eight, I've been in L.A. for three years, and, after a whole lot of working, touring, and honing, I finally feel good about my act. My repertoire of impersonations has grown, but certain ones have become staples—Peter Falk and William Shatner. One night, half an hour or so before I'm scheduled to take the stage at The Improv, I'm wandering the halls of the club, and there's a tap on my shoulder.

"Hey Kevin," says McCauley.

"Hey Jim."

I know him from the several trips I'd made to *The Tonight Show*, accompanying Paul Reiser and Jerry Seinfeld. I hadn't known that Jim was in the house, though.

"Who're you here to see tonight?"

"You," he deadpans unsmilingly.

But it doesn't compute. *Is he fucking with me? Is he that cruel?*

"Are you kidding? Nobody told me you were coming to see me."

"Well, I actually came to see somebody else, but I wanted to talk to you."

"Is this happening?" I ask out loud.

"You're ready, Kevin. You're ready to do the show."

My heart stops like when my mother caught me lip-synching to the furniture. When it starts again, it almost flies out of my chest. This guy's never given me more than a perfunctory "hello," and now he's telling me that he's going to make my childhood dreams come true?

"I'm going to watch you carefully tonight," he says, "and figure out what six minutes of your act to use."

I nod, take a sip of beer, then get hit with one of those ballsy ideas from the ozone. To this day, I don't know where the hell I got the nerve to say, "I want to suggest something to you, Jim, and you might think I'm crazy, but hear me out."

"Um, OK," he says. "I'm listening."

"Jim, I've been watching your show since I was ten years old, back when there was only a small handful of comedians who could stand on the star and even fewer who went right to panel. I know what works on that stage, and what works on that couch, and I don't think, I *truly* don't think, that I'll make as much of an impact from the star as I will from the panel. Johnny does characters and impersonations himself, and I know in my heart that, when I sit next to him and do Peter Falk, it'll have a huge impact, considerably more than it would from the stage."

Nervy? Yes. Ballsy? Absolutely. Insane and career-killing? Most likely. If I told another comic what I did, he'd say, "You did *what?* You shit on The Tap?! Who the fuck do you think you are? Get away from me. You're a dick. Fuck you."

Jim's not moving a muscle. An odd look comes over his face that suggests this is a first for him. Then he does the most unnerving thing possible: He smiles.

This scares the shit out of me, and I panic. "I know there's a protocol. I know you can't bring me right to the couch for my first appearance on the show as a comedian. I know how this works. But I'm telling you, I'm so convinced that the chasm between doing it on the star and on the sofa is so wide that I'm willing to wait until I have a TV show or a movie to promote before coming on. This way, I'm introduced as a guest rather than a comic, and I'll go right to the couch and launch into my impersonations, and I just know that's how I should make my first appearance."

Jim stops smiling, staring at me as if I'm an alien. I see in his eyes that this isn't playing well. So I backpedal. "Listen, I know this is insane, and I'll probably call you six hours from now and beg you to let me do the show as you're offering now. I don't want you to leave this conversation thinking, *That kid is an idiot, and I will never ask him to do The Tonight Show again.* If that's what's going to happen, watch my act and pick whatever six minutes you think are worthy, and I'll consider myself the luckiest guy in the room. Just so you understand, what I'm suggesting isn't from a place of cockiness. Quite the opposite, in fact. It's because I've been studying the show my entire life, waiting for my shot."

He gawks at the alien before him for a few more painful moments. "Well, I don't guess I can disagree with you. Your impersonations *would* have a bigger impact on the couch. But you are also correct that I can't ask Mr. Carson to bring you out to the couch until you have a movie or a TV show to promote. Do you have either coming up any time soon?"

Not only do I not have a role in an upcoming movie or television show, I don't even have any auditions lined up for a movie or a television show. Not only do I not have any auditions lined up for any movies or television shows, but I don't even have an agent who can send me out on auditions. Not only do I not have an acting agent, I don't even have prospects for an acting agent.

I. Have. *Nothing.*

"No, not just yet," I say.

He almost laughs—probably because he figures out what I'm actually saying. Of course, this is McCauley, so laughing is out of the question.

"OK," he says, "if you're willing to wait, great. But let's see how long you're willing to wait. You've got what it takes now, and I can't imagine you're going to get worse. You're only going to get better. The time we're waiting will be good for you and the show, regardless, so let's stay in touch."

I'm elated for a minute . . . at which point elation gives way to nausea.

Now I'm terrified that I've made the biggest mistake of my life. What if he was just acting supportive but really thought I was a wack job? Deep down, he might have been relieved that I showed my true colors early on.

But that's just natural paranoia and insecurity. Healthy stuff, right?

Over the next year, while I'm working clubs all up and down the West Coast and a few across the country, I manage to land an agent. Steve Marks works at International Creative Management (ICM), one of the three most powerful agencies of the day. We meet while he's backstage at a taping of *The Merv Griffin Show*, looking after his client, the great comedian (and my future costar in *Casino*), Alan King.

It's my third time on Merv's show, and at the end of my stand-up set Merv comes center stage as I bask in the applause. He shakes my hand then leads me over to his couch, to my total shock and amazement. Merv Griffin spontaneously paneled me!

Why did I agree to do stand-up on Merv's show but not on Johnny's? Because Johnny can launch careers with a single appearance. While I have deep appreciation for the opportunities Merv afforded me—he gave me my first three television appearances—no one's career started on his show. Other than Charo's. I think.

After the show, backstage again, Marks gives me his card and says, "You should come over to ICM and talk about the future."

Fuck me! That's a great line to a little dreamer like me. Sure, he probably picked it up in a Preston Sturges film from the forties, but I'm about as romantic about that kind of lingo as anyone, so I'm done for. After I sign with ICM, over the next year I go on audition, after audition, after audition . . . easily over a hundred of them. (If you're doing the math, that's one every three days. That's a *lot* of fucking auditions.) Finally I'm cast in a fantasy/adventure movie called *Willow*, to be directed by some small-timer named Ron Howard, and produced by an even smaller-timer by the name of George Lucas.

I call McCauley. He pencils me in. The week the movie releases, I'm ready.

December 12, 1987. Johnny does his monologue, kibitzes with Ed, speaks with his first guest. After a commercial break, it's time.

Doc Severinsen cuts off his orchestra at the perfect moment, and then Johnny says, in that unmistakable Iowa/Nebraska accent, "Ladies and gentlemen, making his first appearance on the show, a young comedian who's in a new movie directed by Ron Howard called *Willow*. Please welcome Kevin Pollak."

The audience lets out a collective cry of *Who the hell is Kevin Pollak?*—or at least that's what I imagined they were thinking—then politely applauds. I walk out from behind the curtain (a move I'd rehearsed five thousand times in my bedroom mirror), wave to the audience (also rehearsed), and unbutton my jacket (also rehearsed) as I step onto that most hallowed ground. I choose not to point to Doc on my way to Johnny as all my heroes have done because this is my first time and I don't know Doc, so who the fuck am I to point like I belong here?

I'm not nervous, but rather as excited as a kid making his first trip to Disneyland, or a kid trying to fall sleep on Christmas Eve, or a guy who's about to lose his virginity. I can't believe this is actually happening.

Johnny, the king, stands at his throne—unlike Jay Leno, who dances out from behind his desk to hug his guests, or David Letterman, who meets his guests halfway between backstage and his desk, then guides them over to the chair. Carson waited for you to join his court. I pass in front of the king and sit down. After a bit of introductory banter, he says, "I understand you do impressions, and you do one of my favorite actors, who we've had on the show many, many times, Peter Falk. Is that right?"

It's customary to paint a picture for the crowd so they know whom you're about to impersonate in case you're not as good as you think you are. Me, I launch right into it, and after two sentences, Johnny completely loses his shit. No foolin'. It was just as I had dreamed when I suggested to McCauley that we wait for this opportunity.

The audience, who always takes their cue from the king, follows suit. If Johnny thinks it's funny, then it's funny—and after only thirty-two seconds, I'm a made man. Afterward, my friends compliment the appearance by saying, "Boy, Johnny *really* likes you." Not, "Hey, that bit killed," or "Man, the crowd loved the Shatner." It was all about Johnny's affirmation. Although he could be more gracious than any talk show host before or since, he never suffered fools. So if he *really* likes you, it's as apparent as Ed's love of booze for lunch. Any booze. And not just at lunch. After that appearance, Johnny has me on the show at least three times a year until he retires. He and I develop a closeness that, professionally speaking, I cherished above all others.

It was everything I'd wanted, and it happened strictly because I took the reins. Had I taken the advice of another comic, a family member, or the agent I didn't yet have, I would've gone on the show when McCauley asked me and been lumped in with every other comic who appeared—not that that would've been a bad thing, but this was far, far better. It was the boldest, nerviest, ballsiest decision of my career, and

Teaching Carson how to do Shatner. As always, he got it down immediately. I actually wrote this book strictly so I could show off this photo. Easily my most prized possession.

it taught me that if you ever have the opportunity to control your own destiny when the stakes are at their highest, *you'd better fucking do it.*

Prescript

The first time I'm booked for the show, I'm bumped because Sammy Davis Jr. sings four tunes. Most of Carson's musical guests do one. Two was the max, and even that was rare. No one had ever performed three.

But Sammy does four. Four fucking songs.

I'm literally kicking the dressing room walls during the third. By the fourth I want to rip out his good eye and replace it with an avocado seed, I'm so out of my mind. Please understand: When you get your first shot on Carson, you call everyone to tell them to watch. I don't mean everyone who's important in your life. I mean, you call every telephone number you've ever written down, ever, because it's show-off time. Each of these phone calls leads to a ten-minute conversation, minimum, because everybody goes on about how they knew this day would come, how monumental this moment is, how great it's going to go, and on and on and on.

Now, because the Candy Man won't shut the hell up, I have to call each and every one of those people back. We're talking hundreds more ten-minute chats that will start off with a discussion about how Sammy Davis Fuck-me Jr. did four songs, followed by "No, they still want me on; we just have to reschedule . . . Well, no, I don't have a rescheduled date yet because this just happened twenty-eight minutes ago."

After the show, there's a knock at my door.

"I am so sorry, man," says Sammy with a commiserating smile. "I know you young comedians work so hard and how hard it is to get this show with the whole sh'konk, k'konk."

All I could do was smile. He said, "Sh'konk, k'konk." He spoke "Sammy" to me and now owned me. I'd seen Sammy perform when I was twelve at the Circle Star Theater—my mother had taken me because she and I thought Sammy was, as she would say, the bee's knees—and now he was apologizing to me and offering to take pictures with me and my then girlfriend/eventual wife/eventual ex-wife.

So, yes, I smiled, stopped kicking the walls of my dressing room at The Tonight Show, went home, and made 114 ten-minute phone calls.

Postscript

Before my second time on the show, McCauley tells me: "Johnny loved your Peter Falk so much that he wants you to teach him how to do that thing with your eye on the air."

When I teach Johnny how to do it, he gets it down instantly. Thank _God_, too, because every time I appear on the show thereafter, as I pass in front of his desk, the king leans over, crosses one eye, and says, "Ah, exschoooze me, I hate to bother you . . ."

Oh, by the way, on that second appearance, on the way to the sofa, I pointed at Doc. Pretentious? Perhaps. But to me it was just acting out a ten-year-old's dream, never stopping to consider if anybody thought me a dick for playing the big shot.

Post-Postscript

A few months after teaching Carson to do the one-eye Columbo bit, I run into Peter Falk in the produce section of my neighborhood Ralph's. Peter kindly compliments my appearance on the show, then says—his one good eye looking at me and the glass one looking elsewhere—"One question, though . . . How do you do that with your eye? Me, I understand, but how do _you_ do that?"

9

Barry's Baltimore

In the beginning, the pursuit of a career in acting is all about handling rejection. During your first couple of years, your overriding thought is, *How am I going to survive?* The onslaught of rejection is such that you begin to expect casting directors to say, "How 'bout anybody *but* you is gonna get this part." When aspiring actors ask me for advice, the first thing I say is, "Don't take the rejection personally. Learning to accept it as just part of the gig is the only way to get from A to B, because it's not always about your talent or lack thereof." Sometimes they want a tall blond, and I never have been, nor will I ever be, a tall blond. I auditioned for the part of Joey Gladstone on *Full House*, but they wanted Dave Coulier. I never have been, nor will I ever be, Dave Coulier, God bless him.

I did manage, though, to land a part in a pilot for a show called *Partners in Life*, later retitled *Morton & Hayes* (more about this later). During the shoot, my agent calls and says, "There's an audition for a Barry Levinson film called *The Family*." Barry Levinson is just coming off of directing *Rain Man* and before that *Good Morning, Vietnam*, so this is a big fucking deal. "You're perfect for the part, but Barry's location-scouting in Baltimore, and they want to put you on tape."

The phrase "They want to put you on tape" is the last thing an actor ever wants to hear. Not only is it a cold audition in which you aren't guaranteed anything, but the director won't even be there, so you're reading for a casting director who knows maybe—*maybe*—80 percent of what the director wants, so when they give you direction it might not be the direction you ultimately get from the director. If you're reading for the director, you do the reading your way, the director gives you notes, you make the necessary adjustments, and everybody's happy . . . which is why the casting director is the last person in the world I want to read for.

So I'm pissed. But then I read the script, and it's one of the best scripts I had ever read and have ever read. It's *the* Jew story, brilliantly written, and if I get the part, it will be the most important part in a film I'd had to that point by a hundred miles. But my hatred of "They want to put you on tape" is so intense that it supersedes my love of the screenplay because I know what'll happen: I'll read, they'll send the tape to Baltimore with a bunch of other tapes, and Barry will have to find time to watch all these tapes, but the only time he'll be able to do it will be while he's in his hotel room, eating a sandwich, returning phone calls, and watching a baseball game. He's not going to focus on that fucking tape. Yes, young grasshoppers, *this* is how the actor talks himself out of getting a part, by pretending that he knows everything, when really it's just a thinly veiled attempt to protect his dainty feelings from pending rejection. Get out of your own way, people. Fear of a bear is helpful. Fear of rejection is utterly worthless. You've heard of the need to develop a thick skin as a way to fight off the rejection. Think of it this way: A man with calluses on his hands accomplished something.

I tell my agent that I'm not all that eager to do the audition.

"This part is being cast in Baltimore, and it's going to be cast from the tapes, and you should play this role, that's all there is to it."

Barry—who had seen my act at The Improv, and always has a stand-up comic in his movies, like Paul Reiser in *Diner*; Robin Williams in *Good Morning, Vietnam*; Denis Leary in *Wag the Dog*; Dennis Miller in *Disclosure*—wanted me to give it a shot. Plus, I'd read for him for *Vietnam* and *Tin Men*, and he professed to be a fan of mine.

Little surprise that when I go to do the tape (God, I *hate* that phrase), my head's not there, and I'm horrible. Maybe I'm protecting myself from the inevitable rejection, and I know it's a waste of time. But hindsight's 20/20, and I was being an idiot.

A couple days later, my manager calls. "Barry saw your tape, and he thought you were really good, but he's not sure what he's gonna do."

"Fuck *him*, and fuck *that*," I say. "I know what that means, and I don't give a fuck. I'm working on my pilot, and it's gonna be a big hit, and I'm gonna be fine."

But when I finish shooting the pilot two weeks later and have time to sit with the Levinson situation and it starts to eat away at my brain, I realize that, even though I don't know much about acting, I know that I can *kill* this, so I call my manager.

"You've gotta get me in the room with Barry. You've got the con- nection"—my manager represented Reiser when he did *Diner*—"so use it. If he hasn't cast the part, I might still have a shot."

My manager talks to Barry, Barry talks to my manager, and my manager talks to me. "Barry's a big fan and thinks you're perfect. He's still location-scouting in Baltimore and can't leave. He said, 'If Kevin wants to fly himself to Baltimore to show me what he's got, I'd be happy to see him again.'"

At that point in my life, with my less-than-impressive bank account, I'm not flying myself anywhere to audition. I wasn't even fly- ing myself to go see my mother. There's no flying myself, period. If I'm flying, somebody else is paying for it, or I'm not flying. But then I reread the amazing script, and it hits me:

I'm flying myself to Baltimore.

I work obsessively on the assigned scene with my *Partners in Life* costar, Joe Guzaldo, and for the first time in my life I feel like a real actor. I buy my last-minute plane ticket to the East Coast ($616, which in 1989 is a *shit-ton* of money for a schmo like me), get down to Baltimore, and go right to the production office—where every- body is remarkably nice to me. Barry and I go into his office, and he says, "You're right for this, Kevin, so let's jump into it. Let's see what you've got." I know he's hoping like hell that I nail it because he's three weeks away from shooting, and he hasn't hired anybody for the role yet.

The scene takes place in a large warehouse, so, to replicate what I think it'll sound like on set, I speak with some volume.

He stops me in the middle. "Hold on a sec. I'm right here. You don't have to shout."

"But in the script, it says we're in a warehouse."

"Yeah, I know, but don't worry about it. Right now, it's just us here in this little office, so the shouting's not necessary"—he laughs—"I can hear ya."

Great. I've rehearsed the thing shouting. But I start up again quietly, leaning into my newly perfected Bal'more accent, and he stops me again.

"What're you doing? What voice is that?"

"I'm trying to talk like you, with the accent."

"Nobody else is gonna use a Baltimore accent. It'll probably be weird if you do, and nobody else does."

For a second, I wonder if he thinks I'm mocking his thick Baltimore twang.

OK, I can't shout, and I can't have a Baltimore accent. These are the things I worked on, so I'm freakin' just a tad. I've got nothing. But in the middle of my confusion and fear, it dawns on me: He wants to see the adjustment. *So make the damn adjustment. What do you have? You have you. So do it as you.*

So I do it as me.

"There you go," Barry says. "*That's* the guy. I'll tell you what: We're gonna have Aidan Quinn here tomorrow"—who was playing the lead—"so would you be open to doing a screen test with him? The chemistry between these characters has to be magic."

"YeahsoundsgreatI'llscreentestsurenoproblem."

Screen testing means makeup, cameras, lights, setups, multiple takes—everything you'd get during a real shoot. I'd never screen-tested before, but it sounded like real filmmaking stuff, and also it will be the first real dramatic piece for me, and I was *so* thrilled to get to the next level.

I learn quickly that Barry Levinson doesn't direct. Literally. Eventually I would come to call him fondly The Phantom. The only direction he gives is along the lines of, "OK, Kevin, you're sitting on this chair, and Aidan is sitting on that chair, and, um, *action!*" He stares at the monitor while you do your lines, then yells, "Cut! That was *astounding!*" (That's his word, *astounding*. Whenever I do my Barry impression for his friends, my repetitive use of *astounding* never fails to crack them up.) Then he continues, "OK, Kevin, you're sitting on the thing, and Aidan is sitting on the thing, and, um, *action.*" You do the scene again, and he says, "Cut! *Astounding.* OK. Kevin, you've got the coffee cup there, and, Aidan, you're sitting cross-legged on the chair, and, um, *action!*"

But Enough about You . . . Kevin Smith

Pollak has that rare ability to give you the best and most believable performance without any director input whatsoever. As such, he always makes me feel even more useless on a set.

Barry is brilliant at writing and brilliant at casting, but when it comes to directing, he just gets out of the way, which is great for actors who don't want instruction, but for someone like me, who's desperate for it—an actor who doesn't know what the hell he's doing—it's a problem. All I can do is trust my instincts.

I shouldn't have worried. Aidan and I instantly have chemistry, and after we wrap, Barry says, "OK, go home, pack, come back here, and don't plan to go back home again for three months. You're doing *this* now."

Astounding.

10

Nothing Like Your First

For a three-day trip, stand-up comedians who do regular weekend road gigs are the best packers in these United States.

Three months is a different story.

When I'm cast in what came to be titled *Avalon*, I have to pack for three months. *Do I have to take all my clothes?* I wonder. *Do I even own three months' worth of clothes?* Idiotically, I don't realize that all you do is bring eight or nine days' worth of your shit, then do laundry once a week. Instead, like a true rookie, I load up two giant suitcases with every item of clothing I own. It looks like I'm *moving* to Baltimore. For the entire shoot, two of my costars, Aidan Quinn and Elizabeth Perkins, bust my chops about showing up at the hotel as if about to set sail aboard a massive ocean liner from the early 1900s, headed to the New World.

As we near the first day of shooting, I get nervous. I want to be *great*. After all, I'm sharing the screen with a who's who of brilliantly accomplished theater actors. Aside from Elizabeth and Aidan—who both had studied at famed Chicago theaters like Steppenwolf—there's Armin Mueller-Stahl, the Laurence Olivier of Germany, with some twenty-five years of starring roles in the theater there, as well as starring in seventy-five films in his homeland. Joan Plowright plays his wife, and she's . . . well, she had literally been Mrs. Laurence Olivier.

A Few Good Words from Kevin's Mom

Joan Plowright had a birthday party in her hotel room, and we were invited to tag along with Kevin. When we walked in, Armin Mueller-Stahl said, "Oh, my heavens, Kevin, why didn't you tell me your mother is such a charming, good-looking lady?" What can I say? A lot of his friends had crushes on me. Maybe Kevin should rename this book *How My Mother Slept Her Way to the Middle*.

Being theater types, they all wanted to rehearse, but Barry nixed that because he hates to see "acting," as he explained it to me later. He wants everything to be spontaneous so interactions and conversations feel real. They all repeatedly ask for any rehearsal time possible, but I'm happy as hell not to rehearse for the sole reason that I'm convinced that if we do I'll be proven a complete fraud—which as a comedian with no formal acting training (just hundreds of auditions under my belt) is exactly what I am, compared to this lot.

"I'm pretty certain I'm in over my head," I tell my manager.

"You know, Paul Reiser just did *Aliens*," he says, "and he was nervous about it because there was no real comedy. So he found an acting coach to work with in private. If you want, it might be helpful."

I'd never taken acting classes because I feared being told by a trained actor that I can't act, so, as a defense mechanism, I'd tell anyone who'd listen, *If they're so wonderful, why are they teaching instead of working?* But I'm so worked up about *Avalon* that I tell my agent that an acting coach would be great.

"I'm getting some help from an acting coach," I tell Barry later that day. "If it's OK, I need to get him a copy of the script."

"Oh, no. No, no, no. No, you're this guy. That's why I gave you the part—because you *are* this guy. I don't want some putz telling you how to be this guy. Just be loose and comfortable in front of the camera the way you were in the screen test, and you're gonna be great. I'm not letting some acting coach in here to screw up what you've already got. I'm tellin' ya, you're this guy."

This conversation is the reason that I become a good actor . . . if I am a good actor, that is. (Still up for debate in some critics' minds.) At my first time at bat, in my first dramatic role, the first time I really need to prove myself to real actors, my director doesn't care about process, method, or any of that shit. He just wants you to be. This is fantastic because all I'm capable of doing is being. Barry's hatred of seeing anyone act teaches me how to be loose, free, and real in front of the camera, which, as it turned out, is all any of the "real" actors are striving and killing themselves to achieve.

I was, it turned out, a natural.

But Enough about You . . . Jim Gaffigan

When I was getting started in stand-up comedy in the early 1800s, there were a handful of comedians that I truly admired and had dream careers. Of course, Kevin Pollak was not one of those comedians. Actually, Kevin's ability to mix within the stand-up and acting worlds amazed me. I'm still jealous. To make a living doing what you love is a real blessing, but to succeed in both stand-up and acting like Kevin is virtually impossible.

Something else I learn is that Barry Levinson is a funny son of a bitch.

Back in the 1960s, Barry Levinson was a stand-up comic. He used to play coffeehouses with then-partner Craig T. Nelson of *Poltergeist* and *Coach* fame. Consequently, Barry always thinks like a comedian. Let me explain.

The most important thing a comic can do is find his voice, his point-of-view. Once you have your P.O.V.—sarcasm, observation, biting social commentary, whatever—everything and anything in your life is material. Me, I'm part storyteller and part social commentator. Barry is all of the above.

This is a guy who can talk about anything and be hilarious. It's frustrating because he puts some gold out there, and then it's gone, never to be performed in a club, on TV, or anywhere other than on that set at that moment. After he'd deliver down some genius run, I'd say to him, "I'm going on Letterman's show next week. Let me do that bit you just made up on the spot, a bit that's going to evaporate unless you let me give it life." For instance . . .

"I think I might've found a way to save the Coca-Cola bottling company a half a billion dollars a year. I was at the grocery store with my son Jack—he's five—and he said, 'Hey, Dad, can I get the Diet Coca-Cola?' I said, 'Why do you want the *Diet* Coca-Cola, Jack? You're five.' He said, 'Because it's less than one calorie.' And I'm thinking, a five-year-old doesn't need to concern himself with how many calories are in a pop. Clearly he saw a commercial that stuck in his head. Then that made me realize the ridiculous nature of 'Less than one calorie.' Why do they have to stress *less than* one calorie? Are you going to sell less Coca-Cola if it just says 'one calorie?' No. So if they stop painting the words 'less than' on every can that will be manufactured for worldwide consumption in this year alone, the Coca-Cola people will save themselves half a billion dollars."

Then there was his bit about *The Silence of the Lambs.* But first, it's important that I explain Rob Reiner's theory of why Alfred Hitchcock's Refrigerator Logic is insulting. Let's use his masterpiece, *Psycho,* as our test case.

Rob Reiner's Theory
of Refrigerator Logic

In the first act of *Psycho,* the ingenue embezzles a bunch of money from her company, then hauls ass with the cash to meet up with her lover. On her drive, she has these visions about what's going on back in town, then she gets tired, pulls over, and falls asleep. A cop *tap-tap-taps* on her window, waking her up. She's afraid she's going to get busted, so she gets back on the road, and it starts raining, crazy rain, so bad that she has to pull into the next resting place, which happens to be the Bates Motel. Norman signs her in and asks where she's headed. After she names the town, he tells her that that's only seventeen miles up the road.

At that point, she should get back in the car. I don't give a damn how hard it's raining—*it's only seventeen miles?!* But if she gets back in the car, he can't kill her, and we have no movie.

Hitch, as he was called in the day, called it Refrigerator Logic because you'd go to the movie and you'd be dazzled by what you saw. You'd go home and crawl into bed, unable to fall asleep because you were so freaked out. You go downstairs to get a snack, you open up your refrigerator and think, *Wait a second. If it was only seventeen miles up the road to her boyfriend, why the hell didn't she—*

So yeah. Refrigerator Logic.

Another glaring Hitchcock example that Rob loves to point out: *North by Northwest.* The guy's given an address to meet somebody, and it turns out the address is in the middle of a cornfield. He's never laid eyes on the person he's supposed to meet, so why can't the other guy just drive up to the cornfield, give the first guy a wave, wander over, pull out a gun, and shoot him in the head? Would that be easier than killing him with a plane? *Come on.* Who in his right mind would think, *Kill him with a plane? That's fantastic! He'll never see it coming! So what if the plane will have to fly only six feet above the ground.* A plane is just about the worst way to kill somebody, but it's cinematic as a son of a bitch. Also, the reason Hitch didn't care if people caught on in the light of an opened fridge was that in his day there was no blockbuster, no tent-pole summer movies. Repeat business wasn't yet a thing. The goal for him and his peers was to get people to see the picture *once.* That's as far as the studio's concern stretched, so that's all the filmmakers were taught.

Again, Refrigerator Logic. But now, back to the *The Silence of the Lambs.*

A few years after *Avalon,* and it's Tom Cruise's birthday party. I find myself sitting with Barry and Rob Reiner, and Rob is having his way with Hitchcock's Refrigerator Logic when somebody mentions *Silence,* after which Rob says, "Don't get me started on *The Silence of the Lambs!* That scene where they have Hannibal Lecter in a cage on the fifth floor of that building? And the cop comes in and Lecter attacks him? OK, Lecter's able to get out of the building by cutting off the cop's face and slapping it over his own. The face doesn't just conveniently *peel off.* You can't pull off a face like a mask and put it on your own face. You can't do it!"

"You think *that's* ridiculous?" Barry says, upping the ante. "How 'bout this. Here's the part of the scene we were never shown but had to have happened. The head of the police department gathers the entire force and addresses them thusly: 'As you all know, the most notorious serial killer in history is coming to our fair city. He's going to arrive on a plane, and we're going to put him on a hand truck and wheel him into the building. As you all know, on the fifth floor, we've built a cage, and I've gotta say: It's a pretty impressive cage, especially considering that we only found out he was coming a couple of weeks ago. Now, let's see . . .' He looks around at the three dozen officers in attendance, and says, 'Wilson and Carmichael, you two will guard Hannibal Lecter. You'll be outside the cage, and you'll keep an eye on him. The rest of us'—the almost forty other uniformed officers—'will be downstairs, watching the elevators. If he gets on that elevator, *we're on him.* But Wilson and Carmichael, you'll be fine by yourselves. We have a cage, and the cage is fine.

"'Oh, I should mention that since we had to put the cage together so quickly, we didn't have enough time to put in one of those slots you would use to slide the food in to him, so when it's time to feed the most dangerous killer alive, Carmichael, you just go right in there and give him his supper. Ya know, you can handcuff him to a chair or something. I don't know, whatever makes sense. Anyway, give him the food, and don't forget, the rest of us will be here on the ground floor, watching that elevator, and there's no other way out. *We're on it.*'"

And that is the joy of being around Barry Levinson.

11

Eat Smart

One of the most important moments in *Avalon* is the big Thanksgiving scene. (If you need a refresher, rent it. Trust me, worth your time.) It takes three days to shoot because we need to get coverage of everybody at the table. That means three days of eating Thanksgiving dinner.

Older actors in the scene have been around the block a few times and know about the dangers of shoving down too much of certain foods during the shooting of a meal scene. I'm new to everything about working on a set like this.

> I go to the production office because I need to mail my rent check back to Los Angeles. Once there, I sheepishly ask if it's possible to buy a stamp. They laugh at me. I have since learned that working on location means, through the production office, you can get *anything*—from stamps to having someone killed.

Plus, I'm starving—so, when we dive into the Thanksgiving scene, I go to town on my plate on the first two takes. Seeing that, everybody throws in their two cents, offering advice along the lines of, "Kevin, what are you doing? You're eating way too much."

"I'm hungry."

"Yeah, but you're gonna have to match your eating from seventeen different camera angles over three days. You're gonna have to eat this much on every single take."

"What do you mean?"

"Really? Do I have to say it again? OK, if you're eating a huge mouthful of turkey when the camera's pointing at this side of the table, more specifically at your face, you're also gonna have to eat a huge mouthful of turkey when the camera's pointing at the back of your head so Barry can make sure the scene has proper continuity in order to edit one angle to another. And you don't wanna eat the turkey because the tryptophan will put you right to sleep. You wanna cut really, really small bites of the turkey and focus more on the stuffing and vegetables, but even then—small, tiny pieces."

"You can't use the first two takes," I immediately say to Barry.

"Why? It was good."

"Apparently I ate too much."

Turns out there's an art to eating in movies. You have to give the impression that you're eating normally, but you have to be slick about it. For instance, you can't have food in your mouth when it's your turn to say a line of dialogue. Seems simple enough, but it ain't easy to time those bites just right; you have be constantly aware of when your dialogue is coming throughout the scene. A lot of people are so concerned about filling up that, if they know that the scene is ending soon, they'll chew but not swallow. There were times when, after Barry yelled "Cut," a dozen actors leaned to the side, and, in perfect unison, spit into the nearest, smartly placed receptacle.

The best tricks, when you know the camera is on you, are to cut your food, or season it, or move it around your plate, or take a sip of water, or put your fork down and hold your glass, or wipe your mouth. In other words, when you're the focus, do everything you'd normally do during a meal other than eat.

Jack Nicholson is the greatest onscreen eater in history. (His character doesn't eat much in *A Few Good Men*—other than the other actors.) After my education on How Properly to Eat on Camera, I become obsessed with which actors make it look like they're eating up a storm, knowing how insanely difficult that truly is. I don't know how Jack does it, but he *devours* food. In *Prizzi's Honor*, for example, he sits down in front of a plate of pasta and *inhales* it. In *Heartburn,* he destroys a couple of slices of pizza like I've rarely seen anyone do in real life. And you just know there were fifty takes of his eating scenes, as there are in any other movie. So how did he do it? The answer is simple.

He's Jack fucking Nicholson.

12

Killing Warren Beatty

My father, as a child, sat on the knee of infamous Jewish gangster Benjamin "Bugsy" Siegel and went to summer camp with his daughters. I also learned quite recently that, when Mr. Siegel made regular trips up to the San Francisco area, he often sat in at my grandfather's poker game. Bugsy's story has always enamored me, so when Barry Levinson invites me to visit the set of his biopic *Bugsy*, starring Warren Beatty, I sprint to my car and shatter the local speed limits.

I arrive at the set and say hello to Barry, who reintroduces me to Warren. I am also enamored by Mr. Beatty. After all, he was the first megastar to acknowledge my existence in film—and possibly on the planet—and he had complimented me at the *Avalon* premiere. "Great to see you again," Warren says. "I shouldn't shake your hand. I've got this terrible bronchitis, and I'm coughing like an idiot." But that doesn't stop him from working. Bronchial or not, he's mesmerizing take after take.

After several takes, there's a break to tweak the lighting, which is something Barry has no patience for. On *Avalon*, he had major problems with his cinematographer, Academy Award–winning Allen Daviau, because Allen took a considerable amount of time to light a scene. When Barry got frustrated with Allen, he told anybody within earshot, "It doesn't matter whether Allen's lighting a football or a football stadium. It takes three hours." But to Barry and every other director with whom Allen worked, it was worth it. Everything he shoots looks stunning.

During *Avalon*, I did a bit for Barry, a huge baseball fan, that had him in stitches. During this break, while Barry, Warren, and I are waiting around for Allen to finish, Barry says, "Kevin, do the baseball bit. I told Warren about the baseball bit."

Warren lets out a horrible cough. "Yeah, *cough*, do the baseball bit, *hack, hack.*"

I don't think about the consequences of making Warren laugh up a lung. I just launch into the bit.

> Before I tell you the bit, there's something you have to know: It wasn't my bit, and I made that clear to Barry, as I do whenever telling this bit. It belongs to a comedian friend named Jim Edwards. I mention Jim because comedians have a strong code of honor—except for certain acts, no reason to mention any names, *Carlos Mencia*—that says you don't take anybody else's material without permission or, at the very least, giving credit. Whenever I do this bit for friends, I always give Jim credit. *Always.*

The setup: We're listening to a broadcast of a baseball game in which the batter keeps fouling off a three-and-two pitch, and the announcer is running out of background material on him. As a rule, baseball announcers are the last "performers" you want improvising. Please imagine this bit done in a voice best described as "classic baseball announcer."

"*Here's the three-two pitch . . . fouled off again. You know, it's a beautiful night here at the ballpark, plenty of stars up in the sky. Reminds me of my favorite astronomer, Copernicus. Y'know, a lot of people don't know he had a first name: Rick. Rick Copernicus—some kind of stargazer. Here's the three-two pitch . . . fouled off again.*

"*Y'know, we had a brawl out in the stands earlier tonight—couple of guys mixing it up, and it reminded me of a guy who could really keep things under control: Mahatma Gandhi. Mahatma . . . had a younger brother, Bobby Gandhi. Played in the minors in Nepal a couple of years—never made it to the bigs. But y'know, the Hindus had to be plenty proud to acquire him in that deal. Mahatma—some kind of leader. Here's the three-two pitch, fouled off again.*

"*Say, did anybody ever see* <u>*E. T.*</u>*? Little fella just wanted to go home, didn't he? Boy, we sure could use him now in our bullpen, with that split-fingered fastball. E.T.—some kind of space creature. Here's the three-two pitch, fouled off again.*

"*We've got the Jewish holidays coming up here pretty quick. Reminds me of my favorite double-play combination, Ma Nish Tanah, over to Ha Lileh, over to Ha Zeh. Boy, you talk about guilt in the infield when they made an error—some kind of Jew holiday.*"

And there's more. Quite a bit more.

After the first big payoff of the bit, "Rick Copernicus," Warren is laughing with such a severe rattle that I think I should stop hurting him.

"Should I go on?" I ask.

"Yes, yes, *cough, hack, cough,* keep going, *hack, cough, hack, hack, hack,* please."

So I keep going. Hacking turns to choking, and I half-expect blood to spew from his mouth. Warren is in ridiculous pain, and Barry isn't helping because all the while he's laughing harder than anyone else. *Doesn't Barry realize that if this doesn't stop soon his star may never work again, let alone finish the picture?* But Warren and Barry keep insisting that I finish, despite that, if I actually do finish the bit, Warren clearly won't survive. So I cut out a chunk from the middle, and call it a day.

A lone gunman's hail of bullets may have killed Benjamin Siegel as he watched a movie from the safety of his Hancock Park home, but I have Jim Edwards to thank for allowing me to almost kill the great actor who brilliantly portrayed him.

Postscript

I did the bit for Matthew Perry while we were shooting <u>*The Whole Nine Yards*</u>*, and he loved it so much that, when he was asked to host the*

ESPY Awards years later, he called and asked if he could perform it on the broadcast.

"You certainly can't do it on TV without Jim Edwards being directly involved," I say.

"Do you think he'd let me?" Matthew says. "Maybe I could bring him to the show and give him a writer's credit."

"I'm happy to call him and broach the subject, but you'll have to work it all out with him."

Indeed, they worked it out. Matthew performed it, and it killed as Jim watched from the audience. Jim got his special screen credit and a verbal acknowledgment from Matthew, along with a wave from stage, as well as a quick shot of him in his seat waving back. I was damn proud to have helped Jim get that kind of acknowledgment . . . especially considering that, if the bit had killed Beatty, Warren's blood would've been on Jim's hands.

13

L.A. Story Story

In the mid- and late-seventies—one of the most impressionable periods of my stand-up life—Steve Martin was a driving force of comedy. He sold out stadiums and arenas, and people everywhere hotly anticipated his *Saturday Night Live* appearances.

By the time I meet him, he's long stopped doing stand-up because, as he explains, the crowds had gotten out of hand. "I used to frontload my set with my worst material," he tells me on the set of *L.A. Story*, "because for the first ten minutes of the show it didn't matter what I said. They were going ape-shit because *Steve Martin* had come out onstage in the white suit and bunny ears, and they were screaming at *anything* I said and couldn't hear a word of it. Finally I thought, let's put the weakest material up front to burn it and the time until they settled down enough for me to speak." He also tells me that he hated working places like Las Vegas, where you could hear silverware clanking.

L.A. Story is the first film in which I work with a comedy legend, and I'm at once intimidated by his presence and needy for his approval. As will be the case with Jack Nicholson on *A Few Good Men*, I don't want to overstep my boundaries by insinuating myself into his workday.

Mick Jackson, the director, is a lunatic—but in a good way. Mostly. A happy lunatic, he's obsessed with how many setups we do each day— "We had forty-five set-ups today! Can you *believe* it? Fantastic!"—so I'm not sure what he knows about comedy. Actually, I'm still not sure what he knows about comedy. He overdirected everything, which directly affects my scenes with Steve. When he gave us all kinds of instructions, I kept thinking, *Why is he trying to make a meal out of a side dish?* Of course, I'll be damned if this nutcase is gonna ruin my chance to enjoy the hell out of this chance to work with a hero like Steve Martin. He's a terribly shy guy, for the most part, but it's genuine, so he gets all the space from me he'll need. Still, we have several laughs about stand-up comedy and working on the road.

At the finish of the shoot, Steve Martin gives everybody the same wrap gift: a lovely, silver Tiffany notepad holder engraved with "*L.A. Story*." He also gave me a card with a joke that I've stolen and used many, many times. The backstory:

Comedian Larry Miller, character actor Sam McMurray, and I share a scene with Steve, much of the shooting of said scene vying for Steve's attention and approval. Turns out, Steve noticed, all right. He gives Sam, Larry, and me the same thank-you card. Mine runs:

Dear ~~Larry~~ . . . ~~Sam~~ . . . Kevin,

You were by far my favorite.
Thank you very much.

—Steve

Of course, Sam and Larry got the same card with the appropriate names crossed out. As a comedian, more so than an actor, being on the receiving end of a Steve Martin practical joke was heavenly.

Sidenote

Mick Jackson's original cut of The Bodyguard *featured only two songs. Two songs. In Whitney Houston's debut film. Does that make sense to you? Yeah, me neither.*

Kevin Costner, who'd won Academy Awards for Best Picture and Best Director, offered to recut the film after Mick's cut horrified the studio. The studio accepted Kevin's offer, and he added eleven more *songs—obviously a wise choice because Whitney's music is one of the main reasons <u>The Bodyguard</u> was such a ginormous blockbuster and certainly why the film's soundtrack became the biggest selling soundtrack in film history.*

Much was made about Kevin Costner delivering the eulogy at Whitney's memorial service. Should Kevin have been the one to send Whitney into the long good night? Who's to say? But considering Kevin's edit of the film and the wholly positive difference it made in Whitney's career and life, who's to say no?

14

The Path Less Traveled

It's 1991, and thanks to *Avalon* I have some street cred as a dramatic actor, but I still have to audition for anything and everything. Nonetheless, I'm happy to prove myself to prospective directors, TV writers, or show runners. Why, I'd even sell my brother for a summer series.

The summer series in question is called *Partners in Life*, eventually renamed *Morton & Hayes*. Created by comedy heavy hitters Christopher Guest and Rob Reiner, the first scene of this odd and original show features Rob standing in a home office, looking at a book. Then he stares at the camera and says, "Hi, I'm Rob Reiner. You may know me from television or film, but what you may not know is that I've always been a big fan of the great comedy teams of the thirties and forties, such as Laurel and Hardy, and Abbott and Costello, and, perhaps my favorite, Chick Morton and Eddie Hayes.

"Recently, while construction workers were tearing down a Foster Freeze to make room for a Dairy Queen, or vice versa, they discovered a vault filled with old two-reelers starring Morton and Hayes that had never been seen. We've dusted them off and will present one of them to you each week." By now, he's worked himself into a chair next to a movie projector. "Tonight's is entitled, 'Saps at Sea.' Enjoy!" He hits a button, the ol' projector whirs to life, light fills our frame, and we're watching something that looks like a black-and-white two-reeler shot in the thirties. The Morton and Hayes faux two-reeler runs for the remainder of the episode, then Rob comes back and says, "Tune in next week for 'Daffy Dicks.' Until then, good night!"

A reel of film is roughly ten minutes long, so a two-reeler is similar in length, conveniently, to a twenty-two-minute television half-hour comedy (after factoring out eight minutes of commercials which, thanks to today's DVRs, you can skip with ease and comfort).

Rob Reiner was coming off the success of directing *The Princess Bride*, *When Harry Met Sally*, and *Misery*, back-to-back, so everyone wanted to work with him. I am also extremely excited by the prospect of working with Christopher Guest after becoming an instant and devoted fan of his work in *This Is Spinal Tap*.

But Enough about You . . . Christopher Guest

I first met Kevin just after he had come to "the big city," as he called it. Like any country kid, he was wide-eyed and, frankly, quite stunned at the hustle and bustle. I did my best to make him feel at home and tried to explain many of the things he was seeing for the first time. To Kevin, girls were "gals," films were "flicker boxes," and nightclubs were "sin pants," which I still don't understand to this day.

But like any gifted person, Kevin was quick to learn the ways of show business, or "sin pants" as he confusingly termed it. In no time at all, his quick wit and engaging demeanor were winning over audiences from North Hollywood all the way to Studio City. His impressions, which are now world famous, became his calling card to the big time. Now that he is well known as an actor and comedian, he has precious little time for the people he first met, but I still cherish the old days when the freckle-faced little *schvantz* sauntered into town with a pocketful of dreams and little else.

The pilot for *Morton & Hayes* is originally offered to Penn & Teller, who pass—Penn needed time to write the foreword to this book—so Rob et al. have to find a comedy team with the chemistry and timing of old pros from the thirties. Consequently, they look at everybody—and I mean *everybody*. Every single man in show business between the ages of twenty-five and thirty-five, every funny-guy, every actor-guy, every *every*-guy. The audition material consists of a couple of scenes that need to be choreographed with a scene partner. It's old-timey fast-talking banter, so there's no room for an "um" or an "ah." Compounding the difficulty, you're paired with somebody you've never met, seen, or heard of, then immediately have to create the chemistry of a veteran comedy team. Everyone rehearses scenes with six or seven total strangers in the non-comfort of one of our apartments in hopes of creating the perfect fit. I can tell within seconds that the much-elusive chemistry isn't there, so I know that much of this work will be a complete and total waste of time.

There's no way I would've made it through any of this if (A) I hadn't thought I was absolutely perfect for the show, and (B) I hadn't already decided that this was the greatest comedy opportunity conceivable. I mean, I just *get* this material. What I don't stop to think about—and what I don't think anybody realized until it was far too late—is that the concept of the show is way too hip for CBS, which had ordered the pilot.

It may, in fact, be too odd and stylized for today's audience, too. The comedic essence and timing hail from another generation, so much so that that style of funny has become, in many ways, irrelevant. Of course, not many saw the success of the 2011 silent film *The Artist*, so I could be wrong.

But the network very much wants to be in the Reiner/Guest business, so there was no stopping to consider whether an audience will tune in. Christopher and Rob are still riding high from the total creative freedom given to them during the making of *This Is Spinal Tap*—which reinvented how to be funny on film—and feel empowered to stick to their guns.

After months of choreographing scenes with person after person after person, they pare it down to six people. Of the six, I'm the only one reading for both parts, so they partner me up with two different people. In one, I'm the clear leader of the team, Chick Morton, paired with none other than Nathan Lane; in the other audition, I play befuddled sidekick Eddie Hayes, paired with an actor out of Chicago, Joe Guzaldo, as Chick.

> I should mention for those not "in the industry," that when an actor gets to this point in the process, he gets a "test deal," which means that his agent must completely negotiate a contract before the audition for the network. The networks do this because the actor is at his most vulnerable, his most insecure before he gets into the room for the final audition, so he'll take less money. On the other hand, the network can't screw the actors over too badly or too consistently because they have to maintain relationships with the agents. It's a case of *You can't fuck me on this one because if you do I'll fuck you on the next one.*
>
> When you go into that final audition, you know that your deal is already in place. You know what kind of a bump you're getting from season three to season four—you have to sign for five seasons—and when you go into that final audition you're thinking *If I just get past this last step, I'll be starring in a television pilot, and I know how much the salary I'm getting will make my year.* All that running through your head, and you have to perform as if stress-free, like a child in a sandbox.

The CBS auditioning theater is small, with a tiny, tiny stage, and tiered seating where network folks sit in total darkness so they can remain unseen . . . which means you won't know whom to blame or fantasize about killing later. Outside in the waiting room, we're like six sharks in a tank, swimming around each other, playing mind games, the kind that you learn as a stand-up. Like when you're waiting to go on, and one of your friends is killing it, and he finishes up, he might come offstage and offer an encouragement, like, "Follow that, motherfucker."

> One night I was standing behind the curtain, and, as the comedian exited the stage after killing, he smiled at me, looked at my forehead, and with sudden concern said, "Whoa, let me get you a towel for that!"
>
> That kind of darkness lives in the mind and heart of the stand-up.

Finally, Nathan and I get into the room. We nod into the darkness and launch into our six-minute scene, a scene filled with 1930s banter, give and take, and timing. I can't stress the timing enough, the timing of a comedy duo who have been doing their routines in theaters and tented fairgrounds for years before they got into the picture business. This is not a normal level of performance pressure for an audition.

Three minutes in, it's clear to us that we're getting nothing from the network honchos. Only crickets. Tumbleweed slowly rolls by. It's the antithesis of what we wanted as a response. This type of silence isn't the norm, either, and it's panic time for this comedy team.

Nathan leans away from me, out of the scene and toward the darkness, and, sporting a giant, wildly enthusiastic smile, says to the CBS executives, "This is going well, *hahhhhhhhhhhhhh*?!?"

It's the worst scene-partner assassination I've seen or will ever see. As far as I could figure, in that moment, with our efforts dying a slow death, Nathan thought, *This is going horribly, and neither of us is getting hired, so I'm going to get a laugh out of these black-hearted fuckers.* Of course, he gets a huge laugh, after which he goes back into the scene, and we proceed to bomb for another three minutes.

The end result: I get hired. Nathan doesn't.

Listen, I understand his panic, and I've teased him about it at least a dozen times over the last twenty years. Course, Nathan ended up getting work somewhere, I believe, so it worked out for everybody.

For the final casting of *Morton & Hayes*, it's decided that an actor named Joe Guzaldo is best suited for the role of snappy alpha male, Chick Morton. Although I'm not a natural at portraying a befuddled sidekick, Rob and Chris love what I did as both characters and ask me to play a version of Eddie Hayes somewhere in the middle of alpha and befuddled. Alphuddled? Befalpha? Hmm . . .

The gorgeous and talented Jennifer Jason Leigh joins the cast as the gal, and Chris plays the heavy. Writer Carl Gottleib, who penned the screenplay for *Jaws*, directs the pilot. (He's responsible for the line, "You're gonna need a bigger boat," a line that I and others enjoy throwing his way at a poker table on those rare occasions when he has a full house and loses.) Carl does a terrific job, but I still wish that Rob directed the pilot.

Even though the pilot turns out pretty damn good, the network passes . . . until, several months later, they decide to order it as a

On the set of *Partners in Life* with kimono'd Jennifer Jason Leigh, fezzed-up Christopher Guest, and my partner, Joe Guzaldo.

six-week summer series. (This turn of events takes place back when none of the networks ran any original comedy or drama series during the summer months, then a long-standing tradition.) Sadly for my pal Joe Guzaldo, the network wants changes in casting. They want me as Chick and ask Rob and Chris to find a "tubby actor" to play Eddie. I experience another painful reality of business as Joe is shown the door and a relative unknown named Bob Amaral is hired to play Eddie. We shoot six glorious episodes of *Morton & Hayes,* but the viewership never materializes, so six is all we get.

Postscript

While I was happy for my series costar Bob Amaral, I've always felt pretty shitty for Joe, a great talent and a true friend. He helped me work on my audition for Avalon to such a degree that I know I never would have landed the part without his acting prowess.

I owe you, Joe, and always will.

Post-Postscript

Working with Chris Guest ended up being the hardest work I've ever done. The reason? He owned me.

To this day, Christopher Guest can move an eyebrow a millimeter, just so, and I'm on the ground laughing uncontrollably. Certain comic performers just get the better of you, and you cannot control the laughter. Take after take, I laughed and blew the shot. It got so bad that I had to resort to what I call forehead acting. Whenever he and I had a face-to-face scene together, I had to stare at his forehead instead of looking into his eyes, or I wouldn't get through it without losing my shit.

Son of a bitch still owns me.

15

Called Up to the Majors

During *Morton & Hayes*, I eat lunch with Rob most every day.

"This next movie I'm gonna do," he says one afternoon, "is an adaptation of a big Broadway hit called *A Few Good Men*." The play had had five hundred performances and was a monster success—but it was just a Broadway play. Most of Los Angeles doesn't know what goes on in the world of theater.

"It's a courtroom drama, and the playwright has written a great script. It should be a good movie. I've got Tom Cruise for the lead."

"Wow, Rob, that's fantastic."

"Yeah," he says, "it's great. *He's* great. I'm getting close on Demi Moore as the female lead, and I think we're gonna get Jack Nicholson to play the heavy, this crazy colonel."

"Holy shit, man."

Rob smiles like he knows how truly wonderful it is and then does something I don't see coming. He waves his portly finger in my face and says, "There's this part of Tom's cocounsel that you're kind of perfect for." (I soon learned that he'd auditioned dozens of other actors for the role, who were also perfect, apparently. But that's the game.) But his pitch takes a bit of a left turn: "I've got an offer out to Jason Alexander, but if *Seinfeld* gets picked up for a second season, he won't be available."

As hard as it may be to imagine now, *Seinfeld* getting picked up for a second season was definitely iffy and leaning toward unlikely. It was on Friday nights and had some of the worst testing cards in history.

> Test audience cards sometimes have the power to kill a show or greatly affect how hands-on the network will be. Jerry shared one card in particular that read, "Jerry is great, but the

supporting cast is horrible, and the show won't succeed because of them." The wonderful irony is that Jerry was the weakest link in that acting talent pool, and the show would never have worked if not for the brilliant supporting cast.

And it had horrible ratings. The only reason that it was still on the air at all was that NBC's late-night division grandfathered it in—late night loved Jerry—so the prime-time division didn't have much stake in its success. It was living on a prayer.

"I'll find out next week," Rob continues, "and if Jason can't do it, you'd really be great for this."

But Enough about You . . . Jason Alexander

Kevin Pollak has taken more than a few jobs from me. I don't understand it, as he is not really an actor. He's a passingly amusing comic who relies too heavily on his Shatner impression, which frankly I do better and was doing long before him. Asking, "What is it like to work with Kevin Pollak?" is the wrong question. The proper question is, "Why does Kevin Pollak work?" When I have the answer, maybe I'll write a book.

I go home that night and pray for *Seinfeld's* success harder than I'd prayed for anything in my life . . . and not because I want Jerry to succeed for his own benefit, obviously. Within two minutes of first watching Jerry, you knew he would succeed beyond all expectations, so he doesn't really need my prayers. Still, *The Seinfeld Chronicles*—as it was called back when its season-two fate was hanging in the balance— wasn't looking like a horse on which many would wager.

But NBC answers my prayers and does the right thing. *Seinfeld* appears on the fall schedule for a full thirteen episodes, and, more importantly, the show is moving to Thursday nights, where it ultimately becomes part of the television sitcom pantheon. Most importantly, Alexander was out, and I was in!

"The part is yours," Rob says at another of our lunches, "but I need you to come in and read with Tom. It's Tom Cruise, so out of respect to him he needs to see the chemistry. For that matter, I need to see the chemistry."

This role is going to cement Tom as one of the biggest movie stars in the world. Even though he still has room to grow, he already launches movies. And careers. That's pretty much all I'm thinking as I drive to the chemistry test at Rob's office in Beverly Hills.

No matter what Rob says, I know that I don't have the part—not even close. I have to earn it. This is an audition that matters. It's the single most important moment of my professional life. On the plus side, the part of Lieutenant Sam Weinberg is right in my wheelhouse, plus there's an Aaron Sorkin script filled with what they call actor-proof dialogue, so I'd have to work *really* hard to fuck it up.

A long, but crucial aside about auditioning: My hundreds of failed auditions teach me that the auditioning process is designed to fail. It suffers from one of the most horrible design flaws in the known creative world.

Fact: The level of confidence an actor has after being offered a part is inversely proportional to the level he possesses prior to entering a casting director's office to audition.

Fact: The confidence necessary to give the director the type of performance he wants and needs during the filming of a scene cannot exist inside the mind of the actor during the auditioning of said scene.

Prior to an audition, an actor creates the disposition, tone of voice, emotional range, if not the entire personality of the character on his own, in a vacuum, often only with the pages of the scene(s) rather than the full script.

"Do you know what they're looking for?" the actor will ask his agent.

The agent will gather *kind of* an idea from the casting director, but mixed messages mean that their communication is rarely perfect. Knowing this, the actor seethes with insecurity but must try to build even the shallowest foundation of confidence before entering the room to face near certain rejection.

Now, let's compare that world of hurt with the actor who's been offered the part. He has all the confidence in the world, empowered by the acceptance of the director who chose him out of ALL THE ACTORS IN THE UNIVERSE. It's the confident actor who comes to the set on the day of the shoot prepared to do the best work possible. It's the already emotionally rejected actor who comes into the audition room riddled with self-doubt and fully expecting to fail. The casting director and the director aren't going to see the same actor whom they'll see on set. I'll even go so far as to insist that the director will gain less than zero perspective about what the actor truly is capable of doing in the audition room in comparison to that same actor walking onto the set having been offered the part. You spend your entire auditioning life learning how to fake that confidence, but it never matches the real deal. Anyhoo . . .

I enter Rob's office, and there's Tom Cruise. His face lights up with a smile that is bigger than the great outdoors. The damn thing isn't just welcoming me into the room, it's signaling ships at sea. He's the biggest movie star with whom I've ever had the chance to work, and he's giving me a toothy happy face that makes me feel instantly welcome in a way that I've never felt in any life or career moment. (Trust me, his fucking smile does that kind of shit to ya.) He's instantly likable and down-to-earth, so much so, in fact, that I would later comment to family and friends that Tom's enthusiasm is 100 percent genuine and not at all an act. It's actually—dare I say it—nerdy.

Yes, dear readers, Tom fucking Cruise is a nerdy dude. A generous, über-professional, respectful-to-all heartbreaking nerd, mind you, but a nerd nonetheless. I can't help but laugh, he's so infectious.

The three of us sit down and shoot the shit. I'm acting as if I belong there, the whole time praying that my nerves don't show.

"I really think you guys will be just great together," Rob says eventually. "Say, for the hell of it, you want to read a couple of scenes. Just to—"

He doesn't have to finish. I know where this is going, and I'm up and ready to go. What transpires within the first minute of our read is so definitive that I know in my heart, in the center of my soul, it's *over*.

I mostly credit Sorkin's actor-proof dialogue for facilitating our chemistry, a chemistry that was undeniable. We finish the scene, and there's that happy Tom smile, blinding everyone in the room. He applauds, and Rob beams.

Me? I shit myself.

It's such a fait accompli that I'm getting the role that it seems best to say as little as possible, knowing full well that I could only fuck this up by drooling out something stupid. *Just smile and say thank you,* I think, which is exactly what I do.

Sidenote

One last example of the flawed nature of audience test cards is the one that Barry Levinson carried with him into a meeting with the studio that would fund Avalon. *He had told them that he didn't want them to test the film, and, when they insisted that it was a necessary and helpful part of their process, he showed them a test card he received from his most recent film,* Rain Man, *on which an audience member wrote: "Why didn't the little guy just snap out of it?"*

16

Reading between the Lines

"Jack Nicholson, Tom Cruise, Demi Moore, Kevin Bacon, Kiefer Sutherland, and I are all represented by CAA, so the studio basically said to our collective agents, 'Your above-the-line budget is somewhere between twenty-five and thirty million. You guys cut it up however the hell you want,'" Rob explains to me during another lunch.

This is important because, unlike *Morton & Hayes*, my salary for *A Few Good Men* wasn't negotiated before the audition, so I land the biggest paycheck of my career to that point. I'm a character actor in a supporting role, but it's nice, so nice, that I make more for this single job than I'd ever made in an entire year. But I'm getting something that they all have but that is still a fantasy: a ticket to the major leagues. When this film releases, I'll be one of the only actors whom the audience gets to discover. In other words, when *A Few Good Men* plays theaters for the first time, I'm like Where's Waldo in this cast.

My agent tells me that Rob wants to rehearse the main cast for two weeks, but, before Tom, Demi, Rob, and I start our two weeks of solo rehearsals, there's a table read with the entire cast. The moment I walk onto the soundstage for said read, I see Rob and Tom Cruise and meet Demi, Kevin, and Kiefer. I spot my old pal Christopher Guest. I'm introduced to Aaron Sorkin as well as supporting actors J. T. Walsh, J. A. Preston, and a few others with initials for first names.

As we mill about, a middle-aged man walks through the soundstage door, raising the bar with every step.

Ladies and gentlemen, Jack Nicholson.

Nobody said that, of course, but that's what the moment feels like.

No posse, no handlers, only Jack.

I've met a lot of icons in my life—John F. Kennedy Jr. and President Clinton, for instance—but I've never seen anybody more comfortable in his own skin, living on his own terms. His gravitas is unquestioned and unquestionable. It's beyond show business. It's beyond stardom. It's even beyond being an icon. It's hard to describe, but his presence feels more like Fidel Castro just waltzed into the room—and Jack is comfortable with that.

After that brief second of *Oh my God*, everybody instantly pretends that nothing odd is happening. Nobody wants to be the jerk who gets caught gawking. It goes from a collective *Holy shit, it's Jack* to everybody saying, "Hey, have you tried the pie?" But his ability to affect *everyone's* behavior just by showing up is more than palpable.

When everybody sits, Rob stands up. "Welcome. I'm so thrilled that you're all here. I couldn't be more happy and proud. This is a very exciting day one, and I have such great hopes for this project." Everybody hangs on his every word in part because Rob has a big, commanding presence. He's not egotistical, but he's physically aware that he's in charge. Also, he knows that as a director you need to let everybody know that they should relax their sphincters because they're in good hands. Cast and crew have to understand that you're in charge, and the fish stinks from the head down, so work hard and enjoy the journey. The more seamlessly that message gets across, the better, and Rob delivered it perfectly.

"This is just a table read," he continues. "I'm not looking for perfection. It's just a great opportunity for all of us to hear the script out loud and to celebrate day one of the process. There's no pressure here. We're just looking to have a good time."

After Rob finishes his little speech, but before he sits down, I—like a lunatic—say, "And *you* are . . . ?"

It was one of the ballsiest jokes that I've ever attempted, given the company present. I don't even know that I'd have the sack to do it today, but the stand-up comedian in me couldn't let it sit. Rob set it up too perfectly. It was easy pickings, like T-ball.

And it killed. Even Rob laughed.

> James Spader once told me that he'd heard about me doing this and used it at the first table read of *Boston Legal* after William Shatner offered a similar welcome speech. It killed for him, too, so, if you've got the balls, try it yourself.
>
> You're welcome.

I peek over at Mr. Nicholson. Sure enough, he's laughing, too. I felt like a *made man.*

The whole room loosens up—for a few moments, that is. Despite Reiner's insistence that we not perform, everybody performs . . . except for Jack. He's so brilliant that he doesn't even have to try. He's instantly perfect. But boy was Rob right about the advantage of hearing that script read out loud by all the actors. It was an insanely electric two hours.

We rehearse on the soundstage where we're going to shoot the majority of the film, Culver Studios, where they filmed such classics as *Gone with the Wind* and *It's a Wonderful Life.* Culver isn't as famous as, say, Paramount Pictures, Warner Brothers, or Universal, but I had never worked in a film *on the lot* and there's something about driving onto a studio lot that makes you feel like you're a part of showbiz, that you're not just employed, but rather an accepted member of the film-making community. I had arrived.

"Listen, performance-wise, we really haven't talked about how I'd like you to play this," Rob says to me the first day of rehearsal. "You did such a great job that day in the office with Tom, so I know you got this, but here's the thing to remember: Jack's gonna hit a home run every time he swings. He's Jack Nicholson. He clears the fences every time. Now, because of that, Tom's gonna have to swing for the fences in order to keep up with Jack. Demi's gonna try and keep up with both of them. Plus, as a woman, she knows she's behind in the count the moment she steps into the batter's box, so she's *really* going to be swinging hard. Kev, I need you to hit one into the gap, ya know? Maybe bring in a couple runs, but really a stand-up double is all I need."

It's the cleanest, clearest analogy I've heard. In fact, it was kind of beautiful, and I'm only a casual baseball fan. I smiled and told him how much I appreciated the insight.

All of which leads me to line readings.

Again, for those without an English-to-Showbiz, Showbiz-to-English translation book, a line reading is when an actor says a line either during rehearsal or a shot, then a director corrects him by way of explaining that he's not getting what he wants yet. Almost all directors will try to do it as gently as possible, but no matter how nice the delivery, the actor only hears, *Don't do it your way. Do it this way. Your way is horrible, and my way is correct.*

Some actors like to get a line reading on occasion so that they can better understand the rhythm or emphasis that either the writer intended or the director is seeking. Most actors, however, prefer never to get a line reading because they feel it undermines their own interpretation, which they believe, foolishly or otherwise, is the reason they were hired in the first place.

In all fairness, there are a couple ways to translate the phrase "line reading" in a sentence: "I was given a line reading by a director, and it crushed me." Or, conversely: "I was all over the map in that scene, and then, thank God, the director gave me a line reading." Still, no matter how you interpret it, a line reading isn't a suggestion. It isn't a critique. It's a fix. And it's almost never great.

There are constructive ways for a director to get across to an actor what he wants. Decades go into perfecting the art of this sort of communication. Actors are like children, and, in order to get brilliance from them, they must be vulnerable. But the moment you scold them, the vulnerability from which their brilliance stems disappears.

So when your more experienced director isn't getting what he wants from a performance, he'll tell the actor something like, "That was great," or "That was terrific," or "That was wonderful." (Remember, we're children.) Then he could say, "Now that we have that level of [insert emotion here] in the can, we have a couple of takes to play with, so give me a little bit less—or often in my case, *a little bit more*—[emotion]. That'll give me some variations when I edit."

That version makes everybody feel like an integral part of the process. After observing different ways that directors give line readings without upsetting the apple cart, I've come to appreciate that it's a fucking art form.

Rob Reiner, an actor himself, has his own method. He says something along the lines of, "You know when you say, 'They picked on a weakling. That's all they did, all right? The rest of this is just smoke-filled coffeehouse crap. They tortured and tormented a weaker kid.' You know that part? Well, it feels like it needs to come from a much deeper place for Weinberg, right? I mean when he says . . .'"

What Rob has done there is to relay his line reading to me by acting out the beat. He's not performance level, but it's definitely the actor in him that helps him communicate what he wants as the director. It's organic, it's passionate, and it's almost sweet because I sense immediately that the reason he's demonstrating rather than explaining is that he's so caught up in the moment. It's rough for the actor to see so much of the scene *delivered* at first, but eventually we learn that this is the way Rob works, and it's not meant as an insult.

Four days into rehearsals—by which time, Tom, Demi, and I have become accustomed to Rob's method of communication—Jack joins our little party. One of the first things we try together is Jack's scene on the stand, the "You want the truth? You can't handle the truth!" moment. Before we get going, Rob says, "Guys, don't put pressure on yourselves to bring a performance level. There's no way to fail during rehearsal. We're going to find it, and we're going to find it together."

So off we go. Jack, cool as can be, starts in with the soliloquy, "You want me on that wall. You *need* me on that wall." Even though he's going only at half-power, it's ridiculous how riveting he is. Of course, I may not be the most objective witness since I'm out of my mind that not only was I attending a command performance by Jack Nicholson but I was costarring in a movie with him. (*Holy fuck.*)

When Jack finishes the speech—and it's a long one—Rob says, "Okay, terrific. Let's do it again, and this time . . ."

Before you know it, Rob acts out a goodly amount of the scene. Five words into his gentle version of giving a line reading, Tom, Demi, and I involuntarily step back a few feet. We'd had a few days to get used to Rob's method, but Jack is coming in cold. We couldn't look away from Rob Reiner giving what was, in effect, a line reading to Jack Nicholson. Eventually, he finishes.

Silence.

Then Jack looks up at Rob and says, "Yes. Well. I guess I'm not there yet, am I?"

Yikes. Without even having to infer that maybe Rob doesn't need to act out the entire scene for the likes of Jack fucking Nicholson, Jack fucking Nicholson is saying—in the politest way that he knows—*Let's not do that again, hm Rob? Because I will rip out your eyes and piss in your dead skull. N'est-ce pas?*

The message is crystal fucking clear to me, Demi, and Tom. Rob, however, is so caught up in the whirlwind of emotions of the scene—and Jack is so powerfully subtle, or subtly powerful, in his retort—that it's impossible to tell if Rob got it.

But I never saw Rob go down that road with Jack again.

Sidenote

Regarding the dreaded line reading, on the set of a film starring the incomparable Gene Hackman, when the director attempted to interpret a line for Gene to say, Hackman allegedly pulled him aside and said, "Faster, slower, louder, softer. Those are the only four words I want to hear from you."

17

Trophies on the Mantel

Much to my utter surprise and delight, these megastars treat me as an equal from the get-go. There isn't even a nanosecond where they're anything less than kind and supportive, and it's almost startling because I expect it to be **TOM** and **DEMI**, and (kevin). I'm not naïve enough to think that I won't be allowed to look them in the eye, but I have no idea that they'd welcome and accept me as an equal.

Still, I don't want to make a nuisance of myself or overstep my boundaries, so I'm always conscious about staying cool. Plus, a frequent disquiet lurks in the back of my head that at some point somebody is going to tap me on the shoulder and say, "We've made a terrible error. *You're* not supposed to be here." So I'm overly respectful. This movie is a big deal to everybody, and I know it, so I'm taken aback when everybody gently teases me for being so damn respectful. They were sending me an unspoken message: *Dude, you got the job. Relax.*

So here I am, rehearsing with one of the biggest movie stars of our day, finally getting over my I-don't-belong nerves, finally comfortable enough to fuck with Tom.

Day three of rehearsal, and Tom's making notes in his script.

> Actors do this because they want to remember a certain stage direction days, weeks, or months later, so, moments after getting an important piece of guidance, or discovering a certain piece of business you like, you gotta write that shit down or lose it to the ether.

But when Tom Cruise makes notes in his script, it's with a pen that's bigger and way more fantastic than what everyone else is using. It looks like a Montblanc on steroids. He's not using this pen to be a dick, and I know that, and I know that everyone else knows, so, therefore, making fun of him would be especially, well . . . *fun.*

"Do they make a bigger pen than that one, Tom?" Then, twenty minutes later, "You're *certain* that's the biggest one they make . . . ?"

He laughs each time, but eventually he gets all super-genuine and says, "Kev, check this thing out. Just write with it. It's like nothing you've ever felt, I'm tellin' ya." He hands it over, I start writing, and within two seconds it's like the pen says, "Yeah, I got this." I'm not kissing ass here: It's insane how easy it is to write with that damn thing.

"It's like angel wings floating above a cloud," I insist to Tom as I hand it back. "Where did you get it?"

"It's made by this company in France and available in the US exclusively at Barney's of New York." This is 1991, remember, before Barney's of New York opened locations in every major city outside of New York, including dozens of outlet malls, also outside of New York.

I continue teasing him about the pen being the greatest, most magical pen on the planet, the whole time thinking, *This really is the greatest, most magical pen on the planet.*

Midway into rehearsal, Demi and I become obsessed with The Pen. She does some recon and reports back that it costs $500—which is the equivalent of a quarter to Tom Cruise, but the equivalent of $5,000 to me, an amount that I will never pay for a pen. Therefore, I will never own one, thank you very little. While I continue to admire it and its ability to float on air, I stop coveting it for the same reason that I don't go window-shopping or to strip bars: If you can't have something, why the hell do you want to torture yourself with desire for it?

A few days after rehearsal ends and we begin to shoot, there's a knock at my trailer door. It's Tom's assistant. He hands me a wrapped gift: a teak, triangle/rectangle-shaped box that houses—you guessed it—The Pen, brand new from Barney's of New York.

Yes, $500 is a quarter to Tom, but the thoughtfulness behind the gesture . . . I mean, well . . . we'd just started working together and had

This is the wrap gift that Tom sent. Pretty damn classy, if ya ask me. Yes, it's on my mantel next to The Pens. Lame? How dare you. . . .

To Kevin,
"A Few Good Men..." and one outstanding actor!
Great working with you.
Love,
Tom Cruise

Right back atcha, Tommy.

only known each other for a couple of weeks. I had no idea that people really did things like that. Even as a wrap gift, which big stars often give, The Pen would've been overly generous. But he knows I love the pen—and realizes that I appreciate it for what it is—so he wants me to have it for the rest of the shoot.

Later that day, while I'm making a note in my script with a basic ballpoint, I feel a tap on my shoulder.

"Buddy," says the none-too-pleased face of Tom Cruise, "where's the pen?"

"Listen, the pen is amazing. The pen is one of the greatest gifts I'll ever receive, seriously. But it's no longer just a great pen. It's now The Pen That Tom Cruise Gave Me. It's no longer a pen I can use. If I use it, I might *lose* it. No, Tom, this is the pen I put on the mantel. Please understand, this is a story I'll tell for the rest of my life, and everyone I know won't have a better story involving a pen."

He nods, and laughs, and he gets it, but even so, he says, "I bought you the pen so you could use the pen and enjoy it. It's a great pen!"

"I know, Tom! But it's The Tom Cruise Pen! Please."

"I get it. But just be careful not to lose it. Don't lose the pen."

Three days later, there's a knock at my trailer door. It's Tom's assistant. He hands me a wrapped gift: a teak, triangle/rectangle-shaped box that housed—you guessed it—a brand-new pen from Barney's of New York. I'm dumbfounded. Speechless.

"Tom wants you to use the other pen," the assistant says.

I promise you, Tom isn't showing off. It might seem that way, but he's not throwing around $500 pens like pieces of Hubba Bubba. It's the best way he knew how to say, *Here's one for the mantel. Now write with the other one, you son of a bitch.*

I still have both pens, one of which I use almost every day and one of which sits on the mantel in the teak triangle-shaped box in which it came, next to the empty teak triangle-shaped box in which the first one came, the one I use almost every day. Also, if not for the World Wide Web, I hesitate to estimate how long it would've taken me to find ink

The Tom Cruise Pens.

refills for the damn thing because Barney's of New York sure as hell never bothered to offer them for sale.

18

Hanging with the Big Boys . . . and Girls

"You excited about the Vegas trip?" Rob asks one afternoon, after shooting a particularly tough scene.

"Yeah, I mean I got the invite from Michael"—Tom's executive assistant and the terrific fella who delivered all those wonderful pens— "but what does this all mean?"

"What do you mean 'What does this all mean?'"

"Come on, Rob. I'm the new kid. How does this work? Do I have to book my flight? Hotel . . . ?"

"Kevin, no. You're going to get instructions, but basically you'll drive to the airport, somebody will park your car, then we'll all get on Tom's jet, and we'll arrive in Vegas, and there'll be limos waiting for us that'll take us to the casino. We'll gamble, we'll have dinner, we'll gamble some more, and the limos will take us back to the airport. We're not even spending the night."

"This sounds horrible," I say.

Soon enough come the instructions: Go to Van Nuys Airport, give the guy at the gate the jet's tail-number, and the guy will tell you where out on the tarmac Tom's jet is parked, which is where I should pull up and park.

> The phrase "We're taking Tom's jet" didn't always mean that we were taking Tom's actual jet. Sometimes he leased his plane out, so when his wasn't available, he had to lease somebody else's. In the private jet world, if you do something last minute, you sometimes have to use a different jet because the crew as well as your jet might be leased out to someone else. It all made my head spin.

My then-girlfriend (and eventual ex-wife) Lucy Webb and I arrive at the airport at the appointed time and are directed to the tarmac. We stop next to the plane and give the gentleman to the left our keys. Let me tell you, people, you haven't lived until you've had your car valet parked on a tarmac.

Joining us on the plane are Tom Cruise and Nicole Kidman, Bruce Willis and Demi Moore, Kevin Bacon and Kyra Sedgwick, Rob Reiner and his wife, Michelle, and Rob's producing partner, Andy Scheinman. There are exactly twelve seats and there are eleven passengers, so it's a tightly knit group, in which I have absolutely no acceptable reason to be included.

After takeoff, Bruce and Demi tell the story about getting married in Vegas, after which everybody discusses their own magical marriage moments. When it's my turn to share, I confess that, although Lucy and I have been living together for seven years, we haven't yet tied the knot.

"We're going to Vegas. Get married there!" Bruce says.

Lucy and I had discussed marriage more than enough, and neither of us had much belief in the institution. Plus, we weren't procreators, so there wasn't that pressure, either. But everyone on the plane is extolling the virtues of marriage and absolutely insisting that we tie the knot on this trip.

It occurs to me that this could be the greatest marriage story that anyone in my world will ever tell, so I turn to Lucy and say, "This could be the greatest marriage story that anyone in our world will ever tell!"

"*Do* it! *Do* it! *Do* it!" my fellow passengers chant.

If Lucy had said yes, I'd have gone for it, but either she was far wiser than I, or she was the greatest killjoy in history because, even in the face of coercion courtesy of Cruise, Kidman, Willis, et al., she says, "Oh, no. No. No, no, no, no."

Instead, we got married at a New York hospital at a friend's deathbed. It was his dying wish. Better story, depending on your emotional perspective, I suppose. His name was Ray Belizzi and, although a real estate salesman, easily one of the most original-thinking funny people I've known. One of my favorites of his gems was when we were parked at a stoplight and a clearly-crazy person pushing a shopping cart filled with random crap moved across our sight line through the crosswalk, and Ray said, "Look, Lu,"—what he called Lucy—"another one that let go of the balloons."

At our destination, four limos are awaiting our arrival. We pile in and caravan to the Strip. At the casino, several burly guys with earpieces and sunglasses meet us. Not a surprise, considering the firepower in our group. Professional bodyguards are a necessity for this crowd, and these guys aren't fucking around. To them, it's a military operation.

There isn't a back door for us, to my surprise, so we wend our way through the main floor of the casino. As we single-file through this very public place, there are huge stars in front of me and huge stars in back of me, and all around us civilians shitting themselves. *"Dude, did you fucking see that?! It was Tom fucking Cruise and Bruce fucking Willis! Holy fucking shit!"*

In the private gambling area, as Rob promised, we gamble and enjoy a remarkable Chinese feast. I alternate between pinching myself and reminding myself, *This is not the way you live. Enjoy it, and understand that it is fleeting.* Within our bubble, everyone acts like this is an everyday event. Which it wasn't, but they were all so cool that it felt like it could have been.

Then it dawns on me that this is an unfortunate way to live. It's magical, but there's an underlying sadness. They don't have security and a private room because they're dicks; they need protection from the United States of America . . . or any other country they're in, for that matter. They will live in the protective glass bubble for a very long time, possibly for the rest of their lives. (This new generation of reality show numb-nuts wants to be famous just to be famous, and they have no idea what it's about. Fucking pedestrians, nay, tourists.)

But it isn't all perfect. There's one scary moment during the trip.

In the private gambling area, Bruce is sitting at a craps table. The table is surrounded, but he's the only one playing, and his money is everywhere. He's mid-roll when he spots me strolling by.

"Kev, throw the bones for me, pal," he says, handing me the dice.

"Oh, I don't know, man."

He's having none of it and gives me a look that says, *Come on, pal, throw the bones.*

"How much does he have in play?" I ask the dealer.

"Never mind. Just throw the bones, baby!"

I look the dealer in the eyes. "How much?"

In unison { Bruce: "It doesn't matter."
Dealer: "Just under a hundred thousand."

My arm freezes along with my heart.

"No, man, I am *not* going to lose you a hundred thou," I say, handing back the dice.

"*No*, you're not going to lose me a hundred thou. Don't worry about it. Just throw the dice, man."

Don't worry about it? *Really?* How 'bout you, dear reader? Do *you* not worry about losing $100,000 and just throw the dice? I thought so.

We back-and-forth a few more times until it's clear that I have no choice. So I throw them.

"Five is the number. Five!" says the dealer, who pays Bruce whatever monies he's owed for that particular number coming up.

I'm so fucking excited about not losing $100,000 for my new pal that I celebrate as if he'd won $100 million. (In reality, my roll probably won him, like, $7,500.)

"You know about Godfather Night, don't you?" Rob asks later in the shoot.

"Of course I do. What's Godfather Night?"

"I floated an idea to Tom that we should all get together and watch both Godfather movies. And you know Tom. He got all excited and said, 'We're doing this! And we're doing this at my place!' So here's the plan: We'll go to Tom and Nicole's—"

"Of course we will." Surreal.

> It still feels name-droppingly lame to discuss this, so please know that I don't think I'm cool in any way. It's just that I honestly still can't believe this happened, so this will get it into the Library of Congress and maybe that will finally make it real for me. Sure, the thing to do here is to act like I wasn't impressed by this sort of stuff back then or to act like I'm not amazed today looking back. Fuck that. Think of me what you will. That was me then, and this is me now.

"—and then we'll go into Tom's screening room and watch *The Godfather*, and then we'll break and have a huge Italian feast, then we'll go back in and watch *The Godfather: Part II*. It'll be the greatest thing in the world."

He's right. It *is* the greatest thing in the world—low-key, relaxed, chill, and fun. Granted, six-plus hours of *The Godfather* and *The Godfather: Part II* is a commitment, but the insanely wonderful meal breaks it up nicely. (Tom, by the way, is generous like that. Every so often before a break on the set, somebody said something like, "There's a special lunch for everybody today. Tom flew in his favorite chef from Louisiana." You know, that kind of thing.) This isn't even taking into account that, after dinner and before we go back in for the second feature, I'm treated to the sight of lovey-dovey Tom and Nicole smooching in the corner of the living room . . . and smooching with *intent,* I should add.

Tom Cruise (perky, as usual), Bruce Willis (unusually mustachioed for *Death Becomes Her*), Demi Moore (hot, as usual), Rob Reiner (Jewish, as usual), Kitty Pollak (Craig's wife, as usual), Craig Pollak (my brother, as usual), and me (looking in the wrong direction, as usual) on the set of *A Few Good Men.*

Then there's the Super Bowl.

Early in the production—when I still can't believe that invitations from over-the-top famous people were going to be the norm—Bruce and Demi have everyone to their huge Malibu home for a Super Bowl party. When I arrived, I thought the head of the on-site valet parking company was going to toss me a red vest and show me where I should start parking the *real* movie stars' cars. Once inside, it's a name-dropper's paradise.

The best moment of the seven-hour party comes during the game. A defensive back puts a particularly brutal hit on a receiver, and at the exact moment of impact Academy Award–winning actress Meryl Streep screams at the TV, "*Stick 'em!*"

19

Is the Car Here Yet?!

While I'm planning my first one-hour HBO stand-up special, *Stop with the Kicking,* I tell my director, the great comedian/director David Steinberg, that, in addition to the stand-up, I want to include some sketches. As the writers, Jerry Miner and Martin Olsen, and I work on ideas for said sketches, Steinberg suggests that we pimp Madonna's then-recent film *Truth or Dare.* In her documentary, onstage material appears in color and backstage footage in black and white, like some twisted version of Oz. We mirror that technique with my stand-up segments in color and black and white when we cut away to the mockumentary of my faux-egomaniacal backstage persona.

In Madonna's flick, she and her dancers have a prayer circle right before they go onstage each night. We parody that scene, and during our prayer one of the stagehands in the circle questions something I say, so I tell him that he's fired and he should get out of the circle. In another scene, the doc crew follows me to the area near the dressing rooms, where a nun in full habit steps out and thanks me for the check I'd given her church. I reach out to hug her, and as she hugs back, I pretend that she's kneed me in the balls, shouting, "What the hell was that?!"

> This was before *The Larry Sanders Show,* and to this day it kills me that I didn't have the foresight to pitch my mockumentary as a TV series. Granted, Garry Shandling is a brilliant writer and performer, with whom HBO was dying to do a series— as was every network of the day—and not one of them was wondering at the time what I might like to do.

One of the gags we plan is, at the end of the stand-up show, I take my bows, then we mock all those fake encores and curtain calls we've seen all the great theater actors take over the years. Somebody would throw me a bouquet of flowers from the front row of the audience, then another person would walk out from the wings and put a crown on my head and a robe on my shoulders, then a guy would come out and hand me a big shiny briefcase, open it up, and reveal stacks of cash. As the topper, the back curtain would open to reveal a new car, replete with bikini-clad model sitting on the hood.

Hey, why not try to get a new car out of this? I had my sights on the brand-new Lexus two-door coupe, a car so new that it literally had just rolled off the ships, and so hot that there was a ninety-day waiting list. The damn thing was selling well above sticker price, so my chances were slim to none.

But wait, I think, *I'm starring in my own TV special, and I have a shot at circumventing the waiting list and the astronomical price, right?* I call every Lexus dealer in Los Angeles and try to persuade each general manager to sell me a car for the special. I tell each of them that I need it for the stand-up special, and his name would appear in the credits, as well as the name of the dealership, and since I owned the special, I could guarantee that it would live forever on VHS so people will see it until the end of time.

Across the board, they were very interested in the marketing aspect for the dealership, and then each said, "I'm sorry, who are you?"

But that doesn't stop me. I know that if I keep at it and go wide I'll find the right G.M. Eventually, I track down a dealership in Tustin, a suburb out by Orange County, about an hour away. After my pitch, I feel the familiar ache in my gut telling me that it's not going to happen with this guy.

"Tell ya what," I blurt, in yet another instance of my big mouth moving faster than my brain. "I'm working on this movie called *A Few Good Men* with Tom Cruise, Jack Nicholson, and Demi Moore. If you sell me the car right now below list price, you can drive it to the set, and I'll make sure you meet everybody. My pleasure, no big deal. Now, I don't know if th—"

"*You're working with Tom Cruise?!*"

"Yeah, and Tom's a car guy. I'm sure he'd love it if you took him for a test drive. Play your cards right, and you can get a picture with him next to the car—for your personal use only, of course. Make a great story, no?"

Nine minutes later, we closed the deal.

I'd never done anything like that before, in part because I'd never been in a movie with the likes of Tom Cruise, Jack Nicholson, and Demi Moore before, but also because it made me feel like a massive ball of cheese. Yes, a ball of cheese. It's the cheesiest thing I've ever done by a million miles, and I know it.

Mind you, I've been shooting that movie for several weeks, and I know I'm not really really overstepping my bounds. Yes, it's cheesy, obnoxious, and self-centered, but I won't be penalized or fired. Besides, Tom, Jack, and Demi don't need to know I've made this deal. In fact, none of them knew about this deal until this very second. I'm confessing right now. Sorry, Tom. Sorry, Jack. Sorry, Demi. Thanks for reading the book, though! And please call me to discuss how I might make this short con of mine up to you.

But Tom really is a car guy, so when I say to him, "Have you seen the new Lexus Coupe?" sure as shit, his eyes go wide.

"That's a *great* car. It's an *amazing* car. It's gorgeous. I just read this article about how its unique shape was designed using wet clay inside a water balloon." He knows everything about the car.

"Yeah, I'm having one delivered here tomorrow."

"*What?!*"

"Yeah, I got a G.M. from a lot nearby personally driving it out to the set."

"Buddy, you're getting that car?!"

"Yeah."

"That's *fantastic!* What time's he coming?"

"I guess around one o'clock."

"You gotta let me know when he gets here. I've gotta take it for a test drive."

"Sure thing, Tom."

My God, I think, *it's all falling into place.*

Next day, at 12:45, Tom knocks on my trailer door. "Is the car here?" As usual, he's excited, up to eleven.

"Not yet, Tom. It's not gonna be here until one."

At 12:59 and 48 seconds: *Knock, knock, knock.* "Is the car here yet, buddy?"

"Not yet, Tom." He's more excited about this car than I am.

At 1:05: *Knock, knock, knock.* "It's after one. Where's the car?"

"The guy must've hit traffic."

"*Awwwww, man!* Alright, let me know when he gets here."

Five minutes later: *Knock, knock, knock.*

"He's not here yet, Tom. I'll come and get you before I even go see the car. Cool?"

"Sounds great! I'm just excited!"

"Me, too!"—mostly because Tom was getting me all worked up.

The guy finally shows at 1:30. As promised, I knock on Tom's door. He bounds from his trailer and sprints to the car. The G.M. steps out of the stunning Lexus Coupe—midnight blue with tan interior, and looking like a beautiful spaceship—but before he can say a word, Tom gets in the guy's face.

"Where ya been, buddy? It's *1:30!*"

No, Tom, no . . . Don't scare the G.M.!

"Yeah, there was some traffic . . ." the G.M. says sheepishly.

"Ya gotta allow for that! You're driving from Tustin! You've gotta give yourself ninety minutes to get here from Tustin!"

No, Tom, no! This wasn't the deal! The deal was, he was supposed to hang out with you for a while, maybe get a photo, but now you're yelling at him for being late . . .

Fortunately, the G.M. laughs, which is a relief, because he could be thinking, *I drove an hour and a half to have Tom Cruise yell at me? I don't need this shit,* and then get back in the car and drive away. With my new car. That he sold under list. And delivered to my place of work in less than forty-eight hours.

Tom takes a picture with the knucklehead, and we go for a spin. Tom drives first, and is *soooooo* excited. As we cruise with Cruise, I feel guilty for all of seventeen seconds . . . until the voice in my head snaps out of it and resumes screaming, *I got this car below list and without waiting two days, let alone ninety! The G.M. personally delivered it to me! I cannot believe I pulled this off!*

Postscript

It's a good thing the aforementioned G.M. never asked me to put in writing that I would use the Lexus Coupe in my HBO special because when I spoke with the folks who ran the theater where we shot the show, they said, "You can't drive a fucking car out onto our stage!"

I did, however, keep my word and listed the G.M. as well as the dealership in the closing credits. I'm not 100 percent cheese.

Post-Postscript

After shooting many days on the soundstage at Culver, we all have to shoot for a day down in Long Beach, which will double for Guantanamo Bay, Cuba, for the scene where Tom, Demi, and I see the crime scene, meet Jack and J. T. Walsh, and then have a not-so-enjoyable lunch with the wacky colonel. It's a forty-five-minute drive to Long Beach.

"You want a ride to work tomorrow?" Tom asks me the day before.

"Sure," I say.

He tells me to meet him at some location but won't say why and we'll go from there.

I show up the next day, and there's Tom standing next to a fucking helicopter.

Tom and I just prior to *driving* to work together.

Once again, folks, you haven't lived until you've flown to work in a helicopter. Oh, with Tom, of course.

Post-Post-Postscript

I was one of the few people in America not surprised (or bothered, as it turned out) when Tom Cruise jumped on Oprah's couch. The guy is unbelievably excited about <u>everything</u>, and he was especially excited about a certain twenty-nine-year-old named Katie with whom he was deeply in love. He couldn't contain himself. It wasn't an act, and it had nothing to do with Scientology.

Listen, I get that it's easy to poke fun at a religion invented by a science fiction writer. Lest we forget: The New Testament was written two hundred years after the death of Jesus Christ. Two hundred years later . . . and without Google. But Tom jumped on Oprah's couch because it's how he's wired. Every day is genuinely fantastic for the guy.

I wish I had that.

Actually, I wish that everyone I care about had 50 percent of his authentic excitement for life.

20

Jack and Mom

My mother and stepfather show up to the set of *A Few Good Men* on the day we're shooting a courtroom scene—which actually is *most* days now that I think of it. When they arrive, the camera is hovering over Jack Nicholson's shoulder, from his P.O.V., facing Tom Cruise. (We shoot Jack's P.O.V. for *days*: Jack's P.O.V. on me, Jack's P.O.V. on Kevin, Jack's P.O.V. on Demi, etc.) During these scenes, I have next to nothing to do, and my main focus is trying not to get into a giggling fit with Demi, who also isn't doing shit in most of these scenes.

Since the camera is pointing at the courtroom, there's no place for Mom to stand other than behind Nicholson's shoulder.

> Many actors like to make certain there's nothing distracting in their eye-line during a given shot. Many on-set breakdowns stem from somebody wanting something or someone removed from their eye-line. (Remember that Christian Bale meltdown? Of course you do. That was all about a director of photography interrupting Batman's eye-line.) This is a legit thing—if somebody is moving around in your peripheral vision, from the side, off in the distance, or, in some cases, behind you, it can really fuck with your concentration and pull you out of the scene . . . or, in my case, mess up your ability to remember all your lines. Moral of the story? If you're on the set during a scene, don't move even a little if at all possible.

Those are the rules.

My mom didn't know the rules.

Mom had visited sets before, but she hadn't ever stepped in my eye-line, which may not seem like a big deal, but remember: Your parents are your ultimate judges and, potentially, your ultimate weakness. That's who's in my eye-line: my judge, my embarrassment, my biggest fan . . . my lunatic mother.

I'm squirming because my mother decides that in between scenes it's OK to get all buddy-buddy with Jack. At first she makes some small comments, and Jack says, "Yes, well," and that's it. Even so, I think, *Oh God, Mom, please don't*, because I don't want to have to go over there and turn it into a *thing*. It's horrifying, riveting, and freaking me the fuck out all at once.

As the afternoon progresses, my mother stops chatting with Jack . . . and starts hitting on him.

> I have to stress here that my mother, like many mothers, is harmless. But crazy.

I wasn't privy to the conversation, and I still don't want to know what was said, but I can tell that my mother thinks that flirting with Jack is cute, so she keeps on going. By this point, Jack can see that it's completely unnerving me, so he shifts his behavior. He starts making a meal out if it, having fun at my expense, engaging my mom, and waggling those infamous eyebrows at me the whole time.

A few takes later, after more across-the-set taunting, there's a brief break for light adjustment. Jack gets up off the stand and strolls over to the table where Tom, Demi, and I are sitting.

"How's it going?" he asks me, eyebrows dancing.

"Great."

"Good. Listen. I was wondering if you might be able to do me a favor. Yes. I was hoping you might be able to get your mom off my *ass*. Think you might be able to handle that? Hmm? She's hitting on me. What the hell am I supposed to do, Kev? Am I supposed to take your mom back to my trailer? Is that what you want? Say the word. I won't do it without your blessing."

My mother and stepfather with me and Jack. My mother isn't grabbing Jack's ass.

I'm laughing so fucking hard. Tom is laughing so fucking hard. Demi is laughing so fucking hard. None of the crew can enjoy it, though, because, unlike us actors who spend most of the time sitting on our asses and yammering, they're actually working.

It was yet another instance of Jack's brilliance and kindness. He sees that I'm too uncomfortable to go over and shush my mother while she's having her fun, and he finds a way to say, *She's not bugging me,*

A Few Good Words from Kevin's Mom

The first time I saw Jack Nicholson, it was like, *Wow!* I had to put my hand over my mouth. I liked Bruce Willis, too. I remember at the premiere party, Bruce came over to me and, after some small talk, said, "I'm going to take Demi home and make another baby."

---

don't worry about it, in the most hilarious Nicholson way possible. He's behaving like my crazy uncle who just wants to make me laugh—and it's magic.

Postscript

I'd been impersonating Jack in my stand-up act forever—hell, I did him on <u>The Tonight Show</u> numerous times because Johnny loved it—long before <u>A Few Good Men</u>. During the shoot, a few of my friends call me each and every day, saying, "Didja do Jack <u>for</u> Jack? Didja? Didja? Didja? You gotta do it! He's gonna love it!"

"Why would I do Jack for Jack?" I say. "Why would I want to be the millionth idiot to get into Nicholson's face and say to <u>him</u> in <u>his</u> voice, 'This is what you sound like'?"

Have I mentioned that my friends are idiots?

21

It's *Chinatown,* Kev

The real shock about Jack Nicholson, though, is how silly and playful he can be. You would never expect the epitome of cool for forty years to be that goofy. I mean, in order to be that cool, people have to talk about you, not *to* you, but he's the most approachable and gregarious guy on set. Even so, I'm completely incapable of injecting myself into his world. I can't so much as start a simple conversation with him. I have such reverence and respect for his talent that I can't do small talk. Plus, I've always empathized with people who get too much attention, and I pride myself on not being yet another nuisance. Jack had been picked over and apart for four fucking decades—I simply can't do it.

Of course since he comes off as the most approachable guy around, everybody on the crew approaches him. Even though he seems perfectly happy, I don't want to be That Guy, so I leave Jack alone.

One afternoon, word hits the set, as well as the world, that Magic Johnson is HIV positive, and it's earth-shattering—one of the first times in US history that the disease had hit a nationally famous heterosexual. Not only are our hearts breaking for Magic and his family, but for the first time everyone feels vulnerable in a way we never thought we would. We're in shock.

It just so happens that within our little foxhole, we have *the* authority on the Los Angeles Lakers, Mr. Nicholson. Naturally, people flock to him as if he has all the answers, as if he knows how it happened. At that moment, more than ever, I don't want to pester him, but I'm in the same quandary as everybody else. I want to *know,* ya know: Did Magic have sex with a Haitian monkey, or what? . . . but I leave him alone.

We shoot a few scenes later that day, and afterward the cast makes the walk from the set to our trailers. To my left, there's Jack, right in step with me. In this moment, on this day, it's just the two of us strolling along.

"Hey," he says.

"Hey," I say back.

We continue to walk.

Silence.

"It's surreal," Jack says. "This thing with Magic. Absolutely fucking surreal."

Silence.

"My head's been in a fog all day, with this . . ."

Silence.

"My mind's all over the place . . ."

Silence.

"It's just . . . surreal."

Silence.

We come to his trailer first. He puts a hand on the door handle, stops, and says, "You wanna know 'surreal'?" He takes his hand off the door and faces me. "I'm doing this picture, *Chinatown* . . ."

As he continues, my inner monologue is screaming, *Are you shitting me?! He's telling me a surreal moment from the set of fucking Chinatown, and he starts it by saying, "I'm doing this picture, Chinatown"?*

". . . So one day, John Huston and I are rehearsing this scene. We're outside having lunch, and as he's saying his dialogue, I see behind him, about thirty yards away, walking toward set, his daughter, Anjelica, who I'd just started banging about a week before."

This is already the greatest story I will ever be told.

"Now, you have to understand, John was like a father to me. Hell, I loved him *more* than a father. He was my world, I'm not kiddin' ya, and I hadn't figured out a way to tell him about me and Anjelica, ya know, bangin'. I had no idea how to even broach the subject. I loved him so much, and I didn't want to upset him if the news went over badly. The man was everything to me. I mean, I would've killed her if he wanted me to, and I was already falling in love with her by then, but *that's* how much *the old man* means to me."

Holy shit . . .

"Anyway, I'm thinking about all this as she's approaching the set, and I realize that John is still saying his dialogue in the scene we're rehearsing. As I come out of my own thoughts and rejoin him in the scene, it's at the exact moment that his character says to mine, 'Mr. Gittes, are you sleeping with my daughter?'"

As my jaw hits the cement, Jack smiles as only he and the Cheshire Cat can.

"Now *that's* surreal," he says, turns back around, opens his trailer door, and just like that—he's gone.

22

Jack in the Voice

Jack Nicholson works on *A Few Good Men* for a grand total of ten days, for which he earns $5 million. Quick math will tell you that he made half a million dollars a day. Here's my question: If you were earning half a million dollars a day, when your alarm goes off in the morning, would you hit the snooze button?

Me? I race into the shower; can't *wait* to start that day.

On Jack's final day of shooting, Rob realizes that he doesn't have everything he needs from him, so he pulls Nicholson aside.

"I need you for half a day tomorrow to clean up the last couple of shots. I'll have you out by noon, and I don't mean 12:02. But here's the thing: I don't have another half a million dollars in the—"

"Robbie, what time ya need me?" Jack says.

"Thanks, man," says Rob, with a smile that says much more.

Next day, Jack's there at seven on the nose and does the last of his work. For the last hour or so, the camera is no longer on him, but he's there feeding off-camera lines to J. A. Preston, the actor playing the judge. Then it hits noon.

"We're done with Jack!" Rob announces "Sorry, J. A., I know we've got a few more takes to do, but I promised Jack he'd be finished at noon. He was contracted to be done yesterday and gave us his time today gratis. We'll have somebody else give you the lines. Ladies and gentlemen, that is a picture wrap for Jack Nicholson!"

The place goes nuts with applause and celebration because everyone loves the guy—not just for his work but for the privilege of his company.

As Jack strolls off the soundstage at Culver Studios and off into the sunset, I think that for half of his time on the shoot—five glorious days—he does that courtroom soliloquy over and over again, from every conceivable camera angle, and he's letter perfect each and every time. He changes it up, sure, but it's always perfect. When Reiner cuts, Jack looks like he's been stoned for three days, but between "action" and "cut," he's flawless—a true clinic. I've never seen an actor turn it on and off quite like Jack. He is without question the coolest person I've ever been in the same room with. It certainly seems like there will never be another human as happy with his place in the sun as Jack.

Also, each night on my drive home I've been doing Jack's court-room soliloquy out loud in his voice. I'd been doing a Jack impression in my stand-up act for years prior, but, after five twelve-hour days of listening to him do this scene, his voice has embedded in my brain, so I can't really help but act it out in my car. Easily sixty hours of that fucking thing under my belt.

"Listen," I say to Rob after Jack's gone, "if it would be helpful to J. A., I'll sit on the stand and do the lines. I mean, I can do them as Jack. Not for laughs, though. I'll give the same dramatic reading. Now, I'll only do this if it'll be helpful to J. A. I'm not doing it to entertain the crew. If he finds it a distraction that this tiny Jew is doing the great Jack Nicholson, then it's a horrible idea. But I've now memorized the thing, and—"

"Oh, buddy, that'd be fantastic," Rob says, "Let me talk to J. A.," and then a couple of minutes later: "J. A. loves the idea and is incredibly grateful."

Then Rob makes the big announcement to the crew: "Listen, Kevin's going to give line readings as Jack, but this is serious. Don't laugh, really, because if you laugh it'll be no good."

The first time we finish the scene, after Rob yells, "Cut!" one hundred plus crew members burst into roaring applause, and it's insane. I've had crowds eating out of the palm of my hand hundreds of times when recreating Jack onstage, but this was way better.

Two days later, during one of our lunches—Rob and I had lunch alone in his trailer together a lot because Jews gather; it's what we do; nobody wanders the desert for forty years unless you like each other's company—Rob tells me, "You know, last night, I watched the dailies of Jack's final day, and he's so good, it's ridiculous. When I got to the part where Jack was doing his off-camera lines, though, toward the end it took me about three takes to realize that it was no longer him, it was you. I'm tellin' ya, buddy, I couldn't tell."

A number of people have complimented me about the quality of my impressions, but that was by far the best.

23

Bang Bang, Shoot Shoot

The phone rings.

"Hello?"

"Hey, it's Denzel Washington."

"Denzel. Hey. How are you?"

"I'm very good," he says. "Listen, we're playing longtime best friends in this movie, so what do you say we go out to dinner and see if we can't actually get to know each other."

This call isn't a total shock. In six weeks, I'll be shooting a movie with Denzel called *Ricochet*. But it's a partial shock because, of all the true, big-time movie stars I've played sidekick to, he's the only one who reached out before filming began in an effort to create some sort of friendship. It's a simple gesture but speaks volumes to his level of professional training and preproduction prep work.

We go to a casual Chinese restaurant in Los Angeles called Genghis Cohen—he picked the restaurant, possibly thinking it might be a particularly comfortable place for this Jew, but I never asked—where we have a three-hour dinner and become friendly to the point that our onscreen friendship will seem real.

I tell him how amazing he is in his justifiably revered film *Glory* and how impressed I am that he made so much out of such a small role. "That was inspiring to somebody like me who specializes in small roles."

"I almost didn't do the movie," he says, "because my agent was holding out for a certain amount of money, and the filmmakers wouldn't move from their line in the sand, the whole time claiming that I was the only person who could do the part." At that point, he was on a hit television show called *St. Elsewhere,* and the ladies already considered him quite the handsome television doctor. "In the eleventh hour of the negotiation, we're still kind of far apart on my salary, so I came up with an idea that even my agent thought odd. I told them, 'I'll take your less-than-what-we're-asking offer, but if I'm nominated for an Academy Award, you give me a bonus equal to that amount, and if I win the Academy Award you give me a bonus equal to *twice* the offered amount.' They quickly said, 'You got it, buddy.'"

He was nominated, and he won. Which meant he earned much more than his team originally asked. Pretty brilliant. Needless to say, the guy with the gold statue paid the check at Genghis Cohen.

Ricochet is a Joel Silver film, and Joel knows action flicks, as witnessed by the *Lethal Weapon*, *Predator*, and *Die Hard* movie franchises. He's a whirling dervish, bigger than life, and a lunatic if and when he needs to be. Before ever meeting him, I note that nobody ever dies of natural causes in a Joel Silver film. They either explode or implode.

> Spoiler alert #2: If you haven't seen *Ricochet* and you'd like the outcome of my character to remain a surprise, skip to the next chapter.

If you're still reading, you clearly know the ending, or you don't give a shit about spoiler alerts, or *Ricochet* (in which case, shame on you), so here goes: The character I play dies of multiple gunshot wounds in the arms of Denzel Washington. Not too shabby, know what I'm sayin'?

As I approach the set on the day I'm to be shot to death, the assistant director grabs me. "You need to report to the stunt coordinator, who's going to help you with the squibs, and then we'll go by wardrobe, where we'll have you try on the two outfits that are rigged and ready to blow."

Squibbing involves little explosive pouches filled with fake blood, attached to an actor underneath the wardrobe. Wires attached to the squibs run down your leg and continue on the ground for several yards, where the special effects technician has them hooked up to a kit with a switch that, when pushed, ignites the squibs, exploding blood out through the wardrobe. I'm a plainclothes cop in this scene, and—since it's a Joel Silver film and nobody dies of natural causes—I soon learn that I'm being squibbed in six spots on my chest and four on my back, a total of ten little explosions.

That's a lot of little explosions for my little body. Too many for my taste, but just the right amount that I'm not going to mention it to Joel Silver and get yelled at.

Today, they only rig two wardrobe outfits, which means I'll only have two takes. That's it. In other words, if I can't correctly act like someone being shot to death in only two attempts, *I am a complete and total loser who's most likely going to get a call from Mr. Silver.*

I find the stunt coordinator, who says, "Since we only get two takes, they both have to be perfect. There's a lot of shit going on in the scene, so you can't just stand there while you get shot, and then it's over."—a pause as something dawns on him—"Have you ever been squibbed before?"

"No."

"You haven't been squibbed?"

"No."

"*Fuck.*" He calls over his shoulder, "Larry! C'mere!" As Larry heads over, the stunt coordinator laughs. "He's not gonna believe this shit." Larry arrives, and the coordinator says to him, "The guy's never been squibbed before."

"You've never been squibbed before?" Larry asks in disbelief.

"No, sorry. I've never been squibbed. Listen, fellas—"

"*Fuck.*" Larry calls over his shoulder to another guy on set, "Pete! C'mere!" Pete comes over, and Larry says, "This guy's never been squibbed before."

"You've never been squibbed before?" Pete asks in disbelief.

"No, Pete. I've never been squibbed. I can't believe it either."

"*Fuck.*"

"Yeah, that's what Larry said."

Eventually, five guys surround me, all of whom can't believe that I've never been squibbed before. Why they didn't work this out ahead of time is beyond me.

The coordinator explains how the impact of the tiny exploding squibs is going to feel against my chest so I know what to expect on the day. ("On the day" is an overused way of saying, "When the director yells, 'Action!'") The coordinator demonstrates by rabbit-punching me in the chest. From only six inches away, it doesn't hurt so much as it surprises me.

"No, no," Larry interrupts. "Let me show him. OK, Kevin, when the squib explodes, it's gonna feel like *this*." He hits me in the chest— harder than the coordinator.

"Larry, you're a fucking idiot," Pete says. "They're not going to feel like *that* at all. They're going to feel like *this*." He hits me in the chest slightly more softly than the coordinator had.

"OK, fellas," I gasp after eight more rounds of this, "I don't know if this is a gag, but you can stop now."

"We just wanted you to know what it'll feel like," the stunt coordinator says. To their credit, the punches did vary in velocity from one another. Sort of.

"Yes, and thank you for your genuine concern," I say, "but I believe that I have a pretty good idea now. I appreciate your opinions on the matter. I'll take it from here."

"OK, let me see what you're gonna do when you take those six shots to the chest," the coordinator says.

"Well, sir, I've never actually been shot to death before, so I guess I'll do what I did when I was nine years old and my friend shot me in the yard."

"Yeah, that's what I figured. Don't do that."

"I was kidding. I'll try it like this."

"Cut that out. You look like you're dancing. Listen, couple things: When the squibs go off, they're gonna be kind of loud, so I'm gonna give you earplugs, and you wanna keep your arms away from your body because some of the debris from the squibs might hit you—"

"Debris?"

"—and don't look down. If you look down, the debris might go into your eyes."

"OK, let me see if I've got this straight: Don't dance, the pops are gonna feel like getting hit in the chest by five guys, keep my arms away from my body, and don't look down."

"Yeah, right. Oh, also, it's raining in the scene, so there's gonna be a rain machine on, and water's gonna be pouring down."

Time to shoot my first death scene. My character is talking to Denzel's as we walk down an alley in the rain, and then John Lithgow's character suddenly appears out on the fire escape about twenty yards away on the second floor of an apartment building. He yells something, we both look up, and he shoots me, right in front of Denzel.

Simple.

Since there are three cameras filming and we only have two takes, there's a lot of precision involved. Denzel and I have a cue to talk, Lithgow has a cue to enter the scene, another cue for Denzel and me to look at Lithgow, another cue for Lithgow to shoot his gun. All while a rain machine pelts water on us.

To sum up: I'm wearing earplugs, so I can't hear a fucking thing, plus I can't see when I look up because there's man-made rain in my eyes, but I can't look down or I might get squib debris in them. On top of which, I soon learn that all of the squibs are so well padded that the crew's chest punches were *not* an accurate example of how an actual squib feels. Earplugs: can't hear. Rain: can't see. Padding: can't feel.

On the first take, when Lithgow pulls the trigger and the squibs explode, I dance like a nine-year-old playing Cowboys and Indians.

That's the take that makes it into the film.

A Few Good Words from Kevin's Mom

When Kevin finished *Ricochet*, he called me and said, "In this movie, I get shot, and I die. I just want you to be prepared." "Kevin, it's make-believe," I said, but he was concerned, and it was just *so* cute.

Postscript

In between every damn scene for which he had to have his shirt off, Denzel does about fifty push-ups and/or sit-ups, creating the illusion of a guy in perfect shape—the handsome, generous, negotiating, Oscar-winnin' son of a bitch.

24

Stealing Arkin's Soul
or
Torturing Reiser, Part Two

Alan Arkin has always been an absolute acting inspiration since the first time I watched *The In-Laws,* arguably my favorite comedy film of all time. What he and Peter Falk do together and separately in that film is nothing shy of a comedic acting master class. When I was cast in the film *Indian Summer*, the greatest news of all was hearing that I'd be co-starring with Alan Arkin.

On the set, I follow him around like a little puppy dog—a subtle puppy dog, or so I thought. I'm enamored with everything he has to offer, and to be in the presence of one of my heroes is truly one of the greatest gifts this life has afforded me. Granted, as I've also pointed out, I'm not one to instigate a conversation, for fear that I was bugging the object of my fanship.

But one day, I cross the line. I'm walking behind him for no particular reason other than to be hanging around him, and he comes to a quick stop.

"You know what, it's a little weird now, OK? It's not funny, and it's not cute. You're a strange little man. You know that I'm just going to the bathroom, right? Well, I gotta be honest, I'd really rather do it alone." He takes two steps toward the john, stops, then turns around. "By the way, somebody told me that you do an impression of me. Is that riiiiiiiiiiiiight?"

I wasn't doing Arkin before *Indian Summer*, but we'd been shooting for a few weeks, and that Zelig thing kicked in, so I have him down, and I may or may not have been doing it for some of the cast and crew—but only to make sure the impression was on track. Still, after working with Nicholson, I made a rule never to do them for them because it's a no-win. There's really no point. They *are* them, so it doesn't matter how good I think I am. They're better. The only time I make an exception to this rule is if the actual person asks me.

"I can't do *you*," I say in my best Arkin voice.

"Is that *me?*"—long pause—"That's not funny."

Cut to two months after we wrap. Alan and I are, by now, close to the point that he's given me his home number. So one afternoon, I call him to see how he's doing because we hadn't spoken in a while, and I get his answering machine. As you can imagine, since I do voices, whenever I get someone's machine, I can be a little bit of an asshole.

After the beep, again in my best Arkin voice, I say, "Um, message to myself. Let's see. I know there was something. What the hell? Um . . . oh yes! Yes, yes, yes. Check on the truck for Tony, and get some dog food for Jesse. I think that's it. Yeah, that's it."

I've never done anything like this before, leaving a message on a person's machine as them. I hang up, pleased as hell.

Two days later, there's a message on my machine: "Hi, Kevin, it's Alan. You know what?"—long pause—"That's not funny. No, I mean, it *really* wasn't funny because there were about nine minutes there where I did not remember leaving that message. So, *ha ha*."

Gotcha #2: A couple of years later, I'm flipping through the channels and land on *Larry King Live*, and I'm stoked because Larry is interviewing Alan Arkin. I stop what I'm doing, I'm going to watch this. Twenty minutes into the show, I remember that the last time I was on Larry's show he gave me the hotline number in case I ever wanted to call in and talk to a guest. I never used it before, but *this* seems like a pretty good time.

"Listen," I say to Larry's producer, "don't tell Larry or Alan that I'm on hold. When Larry goes to open phones, just tell him it's Los Angeles." (If you'll recall, Larry's thing was to say the name of the city rather than the name of the caller, as in, "Rancho Cucamonga, what's your question for my guest, Alan Arkin?") She loves the idea.

Larry finally announces that it's time to go to the phones, and I'm the first caller they put through.

"We go to Los Angeles, hello!"

"Larry?" I say in my best Arkin. "It's Alan Arkin. What the *hell* is going on here? Who is this guy?"

Arkin bends over the desk in hysterics—true hysterics—because he knows it's me. Meanwhile, Larry looks confused and panicked. But he's a pro, so instinct takes over and he presses a button on the phone bank. "Chicago, hello!"

"Still me, Larry."

"St. Louis, go!"

I'm in heaven because the producers won't let him dump the call. "Still me."

Finally, Arkin looks straight into the camera and says, "Kevin, I want my soul back." Until that point, I'm not sure Larry ever really knew what was happening.

But Enough about You . . . Alan Arkin

Kevin Pollak does me better than I do, so from now on I'm going to be someone else. When I decide who, I will not tell Kevin because he will steal that person from me, too, leaving me God knows who. Worse, when I do me, it takes off of my time. When Kevin does me, it only takes him fifteen minutes. So he can steal people right and left and still have enough energy left over to do very funny things as himself. Which he also does very well.

A couple years later, I run into my old pal Paul Reiser, and we agree that, since we haven't seen each other for quite a while, we should share a meal with the wives. On dinner night, I call Paul to make sure we're still on, and I get his machine. Once again, I get that itch that needs to be scratched.

After the beep, as you-know-who: "Hi, Paul? It's Alan Arkin. Listen, we'd love to see you. I don't know what your schedule's like these days, but you could come by. You could visit. *You* could stay for a week. Whatever works out, we'd just love to see you, OK? I think that's it."

At one point during dinner, I say something that causes Paul and his wife to look at each other and laugh.

"What's so funny?"

Paul smiles like the cat that ate the canary. "You just said something that reminded us about this message we got on the answering machine earlier today. It was from *Alan Arkin*. I was really upset that I missed the call because I'm such a fan, so we listened to it over and over again. It's hysterical."

I let him go on about it.

And on.

And on.

"Hey, putz," I say finally, "that wasn't Arkin. It was *me*."

He's pissed. *Really* pissed. *Way* more than when I called him as Peter Falk, so I decide to make light of it.

"Whoa. Paul, relax. It was just a joke."

"I called him back!" he says. "Yeah, nice going, ya sonofabitch. I tracked down his number and left a message on his machine. You're an asshole, ya know that?"

As he's going off, I'm laughing because I love practical jokes, and they rarely go *this* well.

Postscript

When I return home from dinner, there's a message on my machine:
"Hi, Kevin. It's Alan. You know what? You gotta stop this now. Yes,
you see, because I don't know Paul Reiser. Never met him. So this is a
problem now because apparently he's sleeping over for a week."

25

Midget Fuckers, Pussy Punchers, Cock Smokers, and Rectum Rockets

As great as the cast of *A Few Good Men* was, *Grumpy Old Men* is the ultimate it-doesn't-get-better-than-this scenario. *A Few Good Men* has movie stars, but *Grumpy Old Men* has legends. Walter Matthau: legend. Jack Lemmon: legend. Ann-Margret: legend. Burgess Meredith: legend. Buck Henry: legend.

When I was a kid, I wondered how nontraditional actors like Matthau and Lemmon became successful, celebrated leading men. (I didn't yet know the phrase "character actor.") OK, there was a time when Lemmon was handsome, but Matthau looked like a tired basset hound from the moment he was born to the moment he died, yet they were nonetheless both revered stars, just not in the Clark Gable/Burt Lancaster way. To me, they had perfect careers: They got to do the silliest, most ridiculous comedies (*The Odd Couple, The Sunshine Boys, Some Like It Hot*) and the most intense dramas (*Taking of Pelham 123, Slaughter on Tenth Avenue, Save the Tiger, China Syndrome, Glengarry Glen Ross*). That sort of wide spectrum wasn't often allowed back then . . . nor is it today, for that matter.

From the get-go, Jack and Walter don't hold the film's director, Donald Petrie, in the highest regard. Matthau, especially, didn't suffer fools.

I meet Matthau for the first time on the set, right before we shoot our first scene together. Petrie introduces us two minutes before I'm supposed to be playing his loving son. We stand there for a couple of minutes while they're lighting the scene, not saying a word. In an attempt to break the silence, I come up with the worst bit of small talk *ever:*

"So (comma) Walter (comma) the script's pretty good, hunh?"

Walter smiles, then under his breath: "The script sucks, kid. I owe my bookie two million."

I found out later that he wasn't kidding; he bet on *every* game, regardless of sport or season, and it had been that way forever, so he has some great gambling stories.

For instance, he tells me about how, for almost twenty-five years, he and Fred Astaire regularly went to Hollywood Park to bet on the ponies. Walter had a foul mouth and liked to shock people with his language. Astaire was the complete opposite. No matter how much money he lost on a race, no matter how frustrated he became, despite Walter's best efforts, Fred never swore, and it became a *thing*. Walter told me he made it his life's mission to get Astaire to cuss at the track, but he never, ever could.

A couple of years after Walter and Fred stopped going to the track, Walter received a cassette tape in the mail. There wasn't a return address on the envelope, and the tape wasn't labeled, but it had come to his private home address, where he and his family *never* received mail, so he was curious enough to put the tape into the machine and press play.

"Kevin, that cassette was one of the most shocking and hilarious things I've ever heard in my life." When Walter tells me this story, he's seventy-three and had a mouth on him that could make a prison inmate wince, so that's saying something.

"On the tape was Fred Astaire calling an imaginary horse race, where the name of every horse was"—and here Walter looks around and then whispers so *he* doesn't offend anyone: "Aaaaaand, they're *off!* Cock Smokers takes an early lead, with Pussy Punchers coming up on the outside. Here they come around the turn, and Midget Fuckers is now in first, followed closely by Rectum Rockets, and here comes Motherfuck Up on the inside. Pussy Punchers falls behind seven lengths, and it's gonna go down to the wire . . ."

"As shocking as the swearing was, I couldn't believe the *commitment*," Walter says. "He called the *entire* race, a four-minute fucking race. He had to have written out all the names because he had to repeat them as they moved into different positions."

"Do you still have that tape?" I ask.

"Of course."

"What do I have to pay you to hear it?"

"Not gonna happen, kid," Walter says, shaking his head. "I'd never let it out of my sight. My prize possession."

Jack had some nice little tidbits of his own, too. Early on, he asks me, "Are you sure you don't mind doing the off-camera lines?"

For most actors of my or really any generation, reading off-camera lines is a given. (I'd heard that there were certain pricks who used to refuse, but I won't name names . . . Don Johnson.)

I chuckle—like I was going to refuse Jack Lemmon. "Of course I don't mind."

He thanks me, adding: "Marilyn never used to like doing it. Anyways, I always ask."

Holy fuck, he's talking about Marilyn <u>Monroe</u>.

That was the thing about those two guys. Without trying to name-drop, and without trying to impress anybody, every story Walter and Jack had in their back pockets involved the greatest names in film history. But those were their lives, and what lives they were.

Another thing Jack Lemmon always did—and this has been reported elsewhere by other actors—was before every take, he'd say to himself, "Magic time." He never said it as an affectation or to be heard at all, really. I asked Walter about it.

"Dumbest thing I ever heard. Does it every take his entire life, the idiot."

They loved each other, and it was transparent every moment, no matter what Walter said.

Postscript

I have a Zelig thing in me. If I'm around somebody for a decent amount of time, I'll walk and talk just like him. This has gone on forever. When I was a kid, my mother would take me to the movies, and, for a couple of days after, I'd act like the main character. At first, she'd find it cute, but then after a few days she was just concerned. It's a weird problem, and it still happens to this day.

I didn't have a Walter Matthau impersonation in my pocket, but after several weeks of shooting with him, there it was. Now as noted, there's never a good reason to do your impression of a certain somebody for that certain somebody, but with Walter I couldn't help myself.

One afternoon, I turn to him and say, "Even though my favorite movie of yours is <u>The Fortune Cookie</u>"—off the beaten track, and I knew he'd appreciate that—"I think my favorite moment between you and Jack during <u>The Odd Couple</u> is when you pick up the bowl of pasta, throw it against the wall, and say, "Nowwwww, it's garbage!"

Yes, I did it in his voice.

Walter smiles with that basset hound face of his. "No 'r,' kid. It's 'gahbage.'"

26

The Odd Couple Goes to Minneapolis

The tabloids are fucked, and here's one of countless examples of how, like Darth Vader, they care only about the dark side. The example I have for you demonstrates how, by doing so, they end up missing great stories that would've sold more copies than the route they took.

On a long shoot, actors will often rent a house, but Jack Lemmon and Walter Matthau each always wanted the best penthouse in town, so before we all showed up in Minneapolis-St. Paul to shoot *Grumpy Old Men*, their respective handlers went stealth to seek out the best accommodations for their clients. The reason for the stealthiness? So neither camp would learn of the other's efforts.

It turns out there was only one spectacular, amazing, fantastic, over-the-top perfect suite in town—a 3,000-square-foot suite with a grand piano, humongous kitchen, multiple bathrooms, two fireplaces, the works—so their respective handlers are vying for this room. They can't decide who should get it, so somebody initiates a conference call between the handlers and the hotel manager.

"Look," one of the handlers says, "you've got Walter Matthau and Jack Lemmon coming into town, and you've only got one Ridiculous Presidential Suite. What can you do for us?"

"Well," the manager explains, "you may not like this suggestion, but I'll put it out there: The suite has a master bedroom at either end of the enormous living quarters. Is there any chance they'd consider sharing the main space, which is almost 2,000 square feet itself?"

The handlers present the idea to Jack and Walter, who love it. So for the entire filming of *Grumpy Old Men*, the Odd Couple live together.

Now, you tell me that that isn't one of the most heartwarming stories you've ever heard. Ready for the *National Fucking Enquirer* headline on the matter? Front page of the rag: MATTHAU AND LEMMON

FEUD OVER HOTEL ROOM. Did they really think that bullshit would sell them more papers than THE ODD COUPLE ROOM TOGETHER FOR REAL WHILE COSTARRING IN *GRUMPY OLD MEN*?

On a more positive note, Jack and Walter invite Daryl Hannah, Buck Henry, Ann-Margret, and me over to their spectacular, amazing, fantastic, over-the-top suite on several occasions—it's transcendent, listening to Jack tickle the ivories in that opulent room—but the most amazing moment is when they had us all over to watch the Academy Awards.

It's no different than watching it with your friends and family. Some of us are seated on the sofas, some of us are standing and mingling, and Walter sits in an armchair directly in front of the tube, not three feet away, the way your grandpa does. There's food, there's drink, people are making predictions and jokes about the more outrageous outfits. In other words, it's like millions of Oscar-watching homes all over the world.

The Best Supporting Actress award is one of the first presented. That year, the nominees were Judy Davis for *Husbands and Wives*, Joan Plowright for *Enchanted April*, Vanessa Redgrave for *Howards End*, Miranda Richardson for *Damage*, and Marisa Tomei for *My Cousin Vinny*.

Let me name those actresses again: Judy Davis. Joan Plowright. Vanessa Redgrave. Miranda Richardson. Marisa Tomei. Three brilliant Brits, one astounding Aussie . . . and Marisa Tomei.

After Jack Palance reads off the nominees, we all guess which one of the four brilliant non-Americans is going to win. I'm pulling for Joan because I worked with her in *Avalon*, and she was unbelievable. But everyone has a favorite among the nominees, except . . .

"And the Oscar goes to . . . Marisa Tomei."

Like many living rooms in that moment, I imagine, there's a bit of *Wow. Look at that, the funny girl beat the dramatic ladies. Whaddaya know?* But in our living room—since we're all thespians—there's a deeper, more intense sense of resentment. As wonderful as Marisa

Tomei is, and as much as she stole that movie, it was an utter outrage that an Academy Award go to any actress for *that* performance. It wasn't even worthy of a nomination. It was so absurd that there wasn't a bookie in the world who would've taken that action.

As we continue with our *What. the. fucks.*, I notice that Walter hasn't spoken. For that matter, he hasn't moved; in fact, he might've even fallen asleep. As soon as the cacophony dies down, some nine minutes later, he waits for two beats of silence, then, with brilliant timing: "I'll sell *my* Oscar for thirty-five cents."

Not only a hilarious way to share his displeasure, but a beautiful way to tell us how ridiculous we were acting.

Postscript

During the Hollywood awards season, comedic actors, writers, and directors always kvetch about not being taken seriously. That being the case, you'd think we'd have been a hell of lot more supportive of one of our own.

You'd think.

27

The Return of Italian Royalty

Grumpy Old Men is a huge success, so a year later it's announced that there's going to be a sequel, *Grumpier Old Men*. I'm thrilled, because (A) I'm quite proud of the first film, (B) I'm wildly happy to have a second chance to work with Walter, Jack, Ann-Margret, Burgess, and Daryl, and (C) I've said this before, and I'll say it again: Ain't no money like sequel money. My salary from the first movie to the second went from, well, let's just say that on *Grumpy Old Men*, if my salary was a top-of-the-line, gorgeous set of custom-made golf clubs, then on *Grumpier Old Men*, it was seventeen Cadillacs.

As if that wasn't good enough, Sophia Loren is joining the cast. This excites me beyond belief because she—more than Raquel Welch on the *One Million Years B.C.* poster, more than Farrah Fawcett in her own best-selling poster days, both truly iconic representations of their respective decades—was as sexy as a woman could ever be on film. When I finally meet her, she's a vision of Italian royalty, stunning and beautiful, with an elegance about her that reads *calm and class*.

The first get-together with the new/old cast is a table read. When it's scheduled, Walter's doing a play on Broadway with Judd Hirsch called *I'm Not Rappaport*, so my agent tells me that, in order to accommodate Walter, they're going to gas up the Warner Brothers private jet and fly the entire cast, writer Mark Steven Johnson, and director Howie Deutch to New York. In other words, the mountain was going to Mohammed.

We all pile onto this schmancy jet, and the first thing I notice is that nobody's really talking to Sophia Loren. Everybody's welcoming and gracious, but there's a palpable sense of *Dear <u>Christ</u>, don't let it be me who says the wrong thing*. They're all on eggshells, almost as if they don't even know how to address her . . . but that's sort of understandable because, as mentioned, she all but embodies Italian royalty.

Without exaggeration, it's a near-silent five-hour flight to New York.

When we land, we deplane and are limo'd to the hotel, where we're immediately taken to the conference room for the table read. Matthau isn't there yet, so we sit without saying a word, probably all thinking the same thing: *We flew across the country, but he couldn't fucking be here on time? Really?* The silence is deafening—which is strange, in a way, because aside from Sophia we all know each other quite well. It's like a reunion for us, but I guess we don't want to alienate Sophia by being friendly and jokey. Even though it is, for lack of a better word, *weird*, but completely understandable that it's all about respecting Ms. Loren.

Finally, forty-five minutes later, Matthau bursts through the doors. Without saying hello to anybody, he walks straight over to Sophia Loren, looks her right in the eye, and says, with a charmingly evil leer, "Great to meet ya. Love to eat ya."

Every chin hits the table. The silence grows thicker as we wait for her reaction.

She smiles and waves her hand at him. "Oh, Walter."

Over everybody's chuckles, Matthau says, "I'm not kidding. Everybody else, *clear out.*"

It was the most brilliant icebreaker imaginable, and it set the tone for the entire production.

Sophia is lovely and engaging and never stands on ceremony. She has an open-trailer policy and, one day, cooks an amazing Italian feast for the entire crew, topped with her own tenth-generation spaghetti sauce. Best of all, a year later, at the premiere, she reminds me about something that happened on that almost-silent flight to New York.

Apparently during that ride, I found the gumption to tell her, "This is so exciting to have you in the film with us, and I just can't tell you how thrilled I personally am."

"You're very sweet," she'd said. "I just hope people *care* like you do. I hope the public *remembers.*" Of course, I didn't know her at all, but it was obvious that she wasn't being modest or even self-deprecating.

My stepdad, Dick Harlow, and mother meet the queen of Italy (and my heart), Sophia Loren. Yes, that's her lovely hand on my shoulder.

She was sincerely concerned that she had been away too long. Before joining us for the sequel, Sophia hadn't starred in a film in twenty-five years.

"*Remember?* They're going to love and adore you as if your latest film was just last year."

When she reminds me of this at the premiere of *Grumpier Old Men,* an even bigger hit than the first, I had forgotten. "Please. The outcome had nothing to do with what I said. You get all the blame for this, I'm afraid."

28

I, Suspect

Once upon a time, there were two nice boys from New Jersey named Bryan Singer and Christopher McQuarrie. They grew up together, went to high school together, and made movies together. Their first film was a small one called *Public Access,* shot for a mere $250,000 that Bryan and Chris landed from a Japanese grant. It made a big splash at the 1993 Sundance Film Festival, but despite all the attention—which included nabbing the much-coveted final night's Grand Jury Award— the film never saw the light of day.

In the midst of the big festival splash, Bryan and Chris ran into Kevin Spacey. Bryan marched up to him and said, "Hi, Kevin, we're total unknowns, but we've written this movie for you. It's called *The Usual Suspects.*"

"Wow, that's terrific," Kevin said.

Of course he thought it was terrific. Kevin had been around for a long time, about ten years, and he was a not very well known character actor—even lesser known than me, believe it or not. Sure he was a colead with Kevin Kline in a 1992 film called *Consenting Adults,* but hardly anyone saw it, so for somebody to have written a movie for Kevin Spacey was kind of a big deal, and he knew it.

"Would you read the script and let us know if you're interested?" Bryan said.

Kevin read it and immediately attached himself to the project, after which Bryan and Chris went looking for money.

It didn't go well.

They were turned down by twenty-eight different financiers, six of whom said they'd make the movie . . . but not with Kevin Spacey as Verbal Kint. They all had their own wish lists as to who should play the role. Word was that James Spader was on one of the financier's lists of approved actors, and several other actors could have had the movie green-lit, none of whom were Kevin Spacey. Either way, all those money men were fucking idiots.

To their credit, Bryan and Chris told the six financiers who said "Yes, but . . ." that they would not make *The Usual Suspects* without Kevin Spacey. Let's put it in perspective: These were first-time film-makers in their mid-twenties, who were offered $5 million to make their movie, and they turned it down because they insisted that a semi-obscure character actor was vital to the film's success.

Lest we forget, this script that twenty-two of the twenty-eight financiers refused to fund went on to win the Academy fucking Award for Best fucking Screenplay. (Let that be a lesson to those of you out there whose brilliant screenplay is not getting the traction that you and your agent know it should be getting.) Eventually, three different companies threw a few bucks into a pot, and, when Bryan and Chris accrue their $5 million, they begin to cast the rest of the *Suspects*.

Here's where I come in.

At this point, I'm getting my fair share of film offers. Not to star, mind you, but to play second banana. My then-agent George Free-man—truly a terrific judge of quality screenplays—calls and, in the midst of a discussion about six other projects on my front burner, says, "I have a script for a thing called *The Usual Suspects*. It's from a couple of young guys who made a film that got a lot of notice at Sundance, which is not really worth seeing—I mean, it's good, but it's not as great as this script, which you *have* to read because it's amazing."

"Who else is doing it?"

"Kevin Spacey's attached, and I think Gabriel Byrne, and that's it. The director's a big fan and wants to meet you if you're interested."

"Can I see the thing of his that showed at Sundance?"

"Wellllllll, I don't think you should."

"Why?"

"Like I said, it's just not that great."

"Then why are we talking about doing this?"

"Wellllll, they did it for $250,000, and it wasn't really a full feature. Plus it's not getting released in theaters. Trust me, *The Usual Suspects* is really their first feature film."

"Do we really want to stop our momentum and work with a first-time director? I mean, you're not even comfortable enough with this guy as a filmmaker to show me what he's done. Plus, did you say that Kevin *Spacey* is the lead?" I say with transparent indifference. Remember, I just worked with *Jack* and—

Zzzzzzzzzzzzzzzzzzzzzzzzzzzzzzzz

Oops. Sorry. I fell asleep while I was name-dropping again. Anyhow.

George interrupts: "Kevin, I think you've gotta read this script, and then you'll understand why."

"Alright, I trust you. I'll read it. Send it over." Like I said, he's a really good judge of quality screenplays.

> Why, you might ask, is George no longer my agent? Wellllll, a couple of years later he took on a struggling Australian actor named Russell Crowe and a gorgeous Welsh actress, whom nobody was taking seriously, named Catherine Zeta-Jones. They popped at almost exactly the same time, and, since they're both normal, calm, easy-to-handle artists, he got a tad busy. My character actor career was feeling a tad neglected, so amicably we parted ways. Shame, though, because he was the best film agent I've ever had.

When I finish with the script, I instantly know that *The Usual Suspects* isn't just the best script I'd read up to that point in my career, but it's the best script I will ever read. (As I write this in the spring of 2012, that's still the case.) As great as the movie is—and as great as its surprise ending is—on the page, it's a hundred times more potent. I immediately call George.

"You were *right!* It's fucking amazing. How interested in me is Bryan Singer?"

"He's a huge fan and wants to meet with you about playing one of the parts."

"Which part?"

"I don't know. And he doesn't know. Just go meet with him."

"So there's no offer."

Since *A Few Good Men,* I haven't had to audition. Have I mentioned that I hate the audition process?

"Kevin," George says, "I know we're in an offer-only world, but this isn't an audition. All he wants to do is discuss the movie."

"Great!" I say. "Set it up."

A couple of days later, I go to Bryan's modest production offices—which, even though he'd just settled in, look pretty tired—and there's Bryan. After we shake hands, he says, "I think what you did in *A Few Good Men* was phenomenal. I know you as a comedian, and I loved *Avalon.* But let me ask you this: What part are you attracted to?"

"What's been cast? I know about Spacey and Gabriel Byrne."

"Gabriel's gonna play Keaton," Bryan begins in his charmingly hyper fashion, "and we just signed Stephen Baldwin to play McManus, and Pete Postlethwaite is playing Kobayashi, and Chazz Palminteri is playing Dave Kujan. So the only two parts left are Fenster and Hockney."

On the page, the Fenster role is nothing—any comedic elements came directly from Benicio Del Toro, who made the most ridiculous, brilliant choices, and stole every scene he was in (more about that later)—but I decide it's best not to point that out. Now, when you take in my little dissection below, you have to ignore everything you already know about the movie because, at that point, there was no movie—just a script. Seriously, on the page, the Fenster role was meatless.

"Well, I don't want to play Fenster because his only function in the ensemble, as I understand it, is to die so that the other suspects know they can never run from Keyser Söze, and he's McManus's sidekick, so I'm not sure there's enough meat there to interest me. I think Hockney makes sen—"

"Listen, I love your work, but Hockney, well, that's something I've not seen you do. You know, a *sociopath*. He's a real honest-to-goodness badass who'd rather kill his way out of a jam than think his way out. Is this something you really think you can handle?"

"Yes, and I would love to prove it to you and the world at large. I went to high school with a guy who was a sociopath at sixteen. At the teen club dances, when he walked in, everyone was instantly afraid. I remember at one point, he stopped by me and my friends, and addressed us about, I don't know, something, and it dawned on me that he had the ability to look *through* you. He wasn't really focusing on our eyes as he talked to us, the way a normal person would. And it wasn't like he couldn't focus because he was high or drunk; he just gave off this still, calm, extraordinarily violent vibe, and I thought he was gonna kill us. He's my inspiration for this. That's what I want to bring to this part."

Bryan smiles like a schoolboy who'd just seen the teacher's cleavage for the first time. We discuss how he plans to shoot the film and part ways.

Instantly, getting this part is the only thing I care about in this world. The next day, I call George. "Well? Well? Well? What the fuck is going on with *Suspects?*"

"Bryan's putting the pieces of the puzzle together, and right now he told me he's trying to figure out the Fenster role. He loves you and wants you to do it, but he can't quite commit."

"What the fuck does that mean, '*can't quite commit*'?"

"I don't know, other than he's not 100 percent that you're his Hockney. Believe me, I'm on this every day. We've got to get this. The moment I find out more, I'll call you."

A couple more days go by, and George calls to tell me that the real reason that Bryan can't commit is that he's already agreed to audition a couple of other actors for the part, and, until those actors have a chance to come in, he feels it really isn't fair to them—or, for that matter, to him—to make a final decision.

"So after they audition, he's definitely going to offer me the part? Or he's going to audition them, and they could get the part?"

"No, no, no, no, no. They're going to audition, then he's giving you the part. It's yours."

"Right. Tell Bryan I'm coming in to audition."

"No, no, no, no, no. You don't want to do that."

"Why would I not want to do that? Why would I want to let another actor come in and blow him away and steal the part from me? You can't guarantee I'm getting it."

"Kevin, I'm telling you, we've had a conversation, the part is yours."

"I don't want to hear this. Tell Bryan I'm coming in to audition."

"Kevin, you're in the offer-only world!" George says, exasperated. "It's a very difficult world to get into, and it's even more difficult to get *back* into. You don't want word to get out that you're willing to audition because that undermines *everything*. When a director and a casting director meet to discuss a film, and they go down the list of who's gonna play what role, and the casting agent says, 'What about Kevin Pollak?' the director will say, 'Can we get him?' and the casting agent will say, 'You gotta make him an offer,' and that's one thing. But if the casting agent says, 'He'll come in and audition,' that's a whole other thing. Once you get into the offer-only world, you're home free! It's the greatest place to be. And you've earned it, plus it gives us the advantage in the negotiation. And you're reaping the benefits, and it's fantastic! Please trust me on this."

"George, I trust you. You know how this game works *way* better than I do. I'm thrilled beyond belief to be in the offer-only world. But I cannot allow there to be the remotest possibility that an actor's gonna come in and blow Bryan away, and then, because we sat back in the Ivory Tower of Offer Only, I don't get hired. If I go in and I don't do well, I shouldn't have the fucking part anyhow."

The upshot: If I wait around, as George has suggested, I have a decent shot of getting the part. If I suck in the audition, I have *no* chance of getting the part. But it's a gamble I have to take, and there's one reason: I know in my heart of hearts that this is the most ass-kicking, mutha-fuckin' greatest script at which I may ever get a shot. Still, I haven't auditioned in a couple of years, and it's pretty fucking scary . . . No, it's *really* fucking scary.

But fuck it. I audition.

I read the scene when we, the suspects, find Fenster dead in the sandy cave off the beach at night. I give it everything in my arsenal and even end up caught up in the moment and improvise a bit. It seems to go well. As I drive home, I'm exhilarated that I didn't blow it; in fact, I feel like I did the absolute best I could. It's always important in these unnerving drives home to believe you left it all on the court, as the kids say.

A quick word about my improvisation during the filming of *The Usual Suspects:* Several of the moments in the film quoted back to me by you and your friends are improvisations, for example: In the interrogation scene, when the cop tells me he can put me in Queens on the night of the robbery, while my scripted response was supposed to be, "I live in Queens, genius," my improvised line that's in the film is, "I live in Queens, Einstein. You put that together yourself? Whaddaya got a team of monkeys working around the clock?"

Another small moment—which I particularly enjoy when people notice—is early on in the film when I'm in my garage, screwing on the side mirror, and the large garage door swings open, after which half a dozen officers rush me with guns drawn. There was no dialogue written for that; I was just supposed to notice them, then, without looking too terribly concerned, reach under the car and grab a rag to wipe my hands. On the third or fourth take of doing it exactly as written, I add a more purposeful glance at the six cops in the side mirror, then say, "You sure you brought enough guys?"

To this very day, I tease the fuck out of Chris McQuarrie about those and at least a half dozen of my other quotable improvised lines that made it into the finished film, saying, "How about you let me put the Oscar on my mantel for just *one week* out of each year?" He laughs, and I keep at him. "Come on, fucker. *One* week, ya shitbag." He was twenty-six when he took home that gold, by the way.

Fucking genius punk.

But Enough about You . . . Christopher McQuarrie

The place: the Hyatt Hotel on Sunset Boulevard. The event: an impromptu bachelor party. The evening's entertainment: acquired on short notice. In a perverse version of stone soup, a hotel room had been hastily converted into a fully working bar, and a Los Angeles police officer arrived with a bag of sex toys for the part-time porn star one resourceful journalist had scrounged up. Things quickly went from bad to worse.

The porn star confessed to a predilection for "water sports" and was demonstrating her considerable talents off the hotel balcony. Later that evening, a particularly drunken reveler asked for a lap dance. Another less-drunken reveler had the bright idea to up the ante, slipping the porn star an extra hundred dollars. Midway through her dance—to the delight of everyone present—the porn star hauled up and urinated on the drunken reveler's head. In the next instant—to the horror of everyone present—the drunken reveler threw his head back and opened his mouth. A camera bulb flashed to capture the moment as the crowd parted Red Sea–like. Grown men fled in disgust, revealing the spectacle to Kevin Pollak, chatting quietly in the back of the room.

With a cigar between his teeth, Kevin said, without blinking, "Well, there's a guy who should never run for office."

On the way home, I call George. "It went fantastically. Now, you have got to get me an answer, really. Come on, now, I'm not gonna wait for him to see any other actors before giving us an answer based on my audition. You have to tell him, George, to make us an offer *now* or to let me get on with my life."

The offer for the best part I've had the great privilege to play made its way to me before I even reached my driveway.

29

The Usual Fucking Cocksuckers

The first scene we shoot in *The Usual Suspects* is the moment in which all the suspects are in the holding cell. During the first take, there's Benicio, lying down on his back, mumbling . . . something. It was then that I decided to do something I rarely do: Ruin a take with a joke.

"What the fuck did he just say?"

Bear in mind that the question came from me, Kevin Pollak, not my character, Todd Hockney, because I think that Benicio Del Toro has already ruined the take. I figure I'm just saying what everybody else is thinking.

Bryan strolls over. "Yeah, Benicio and I talked about his character, and we decided that Fenster is going to speak his own language. It's English, but it's cryptic."

I pull Bryan aside. "Sir, back in our first meeting, remember I told you that I wanted to play Hockney because the only reason for Fenster to live is to die, and most of his dialogue is meaningless? You're saying that the actor you chose to play the part agrees with that and is basically throwing out *all* the dialogue."

"Yeah. It's cool, isn't it?"

"It's fucking genius—and I clearly made the wrong choice."

Bryan then asks me to add my ad lib, *What the fuck did he just say?* into each take. It makes it into the movie.

Yessss.

During filming, Kevin Spacey and Bryan carefully craft a couple of moments that add a layer you won't realize is there until you've seen the film more than once.

I've had more gun enthusiasts tell me over the years that holding a weapon like this, sideways, is the worst possible position for accuracy. Accuracy, shmaccuracy—I was just trying like hell to look cool.

> Spoiler alert #3: If you haven't seen the film—and, seriously, if you haven't, what the fuck is wrong with you?—skip to the next chapter. You're welcome.

When we first see Verbal Kint, he's alone in Dave Kujan's office waiting for Kujan—played by the great Chazz Palminteri—to come in and begin his questioning. Verbal sits, looking bored, giving the bulletin board behind Kujan's desk a seemingly casual glance. The first time you see the movie, you think absolutely nothing of it, but the second time you can see clear as day that he's studying the board so he can incorporate bits of the info into the story that he's about to invent. They purposely design the shot so Spacey's expression will create one emotion in the audience on the first viewing, then a wholly different emotion on the second. They work methodically on moments like this, and it's pretty damn cool knowing what the effects of it will be later.

> Fun side note: Although McQuarrie and Bryan created the film's entire story and characters together, they still argue to this day about how much of the story was fabricated by Verbal from the names and places on the bulletin board and how many of the details in his story actually happened.

Arguably the most famous, most beloved scene in the movie is when the suspects are lined up in the police station and forced to read a sentence from a card: "Gimme the keys, you fucking cocksucker."

I'm the first suspect to read the card, and I read it exactly as written, directed, and intended. Each of us, in fact, is supposed to convey to the cops that we're not intimidated by the arrest. It's supposed to be a big "fuck you," and I believe that I successfully delivered that first take as such.

I cannot say the same for any of my coworkers.

I hand the card over to Stephen Baldwin, who does this crazy guy wagging-his-tongue thing—"Gimme the keys, you fucking cock-sucker, *lahhllhhahhllahhaahllh!*"—which isn't in the script, but which cracks us all up.

It goes downhill from there, and what I mean by downhill is that we cannot get through that scene without laughing.

Benicio farts four takes in a row—which isn't easy given that you have to pace yourself—and Bryan has to change camera angles so we can have a little time to collect ourselves. We start again, and Gabriel laughs at something Baldwin or Benicio said or did an hour ago.

This goes on until lunch. We break for our midday meal, having shot not a single usable take due to uncontrollable laughter.

We suspects have lunch together every day. That afternoon, however, Bryan joins the table. He glares at us silently for a bit.

"You guys are fucking me. You know that, right? You realize I have nothing. We've shot half a day, and I can't use a single fucking frame.

**The police lineup scene from *The Usual Suspects*. I swear, I was *not*
stoned. I was tired from laughing my ass off for twelve hours while we
tried to get one usable take. *What the fuck did he just say?***

I honestly can't use *any of it*. You've gotta get back in there after you
all eat and do the fucking scene right and without laughing, for fuck
sake."

Publicity shot from *The Usual Suspects*. This is when I got up in Baldwin's face—well, his cheek—and said, "You wanna dance?" It's also the moment in the film that still makes my lifelong friends laugh the hardest because they know my true level of toughness.

We apologize to him like crazy, each of us weighing in on how bad we feel, and how sorry we are, but this reprimand is like telling a five-year-old to not laugh during a funeral. You can't say that to a child and expect anything *other* than laughter, can you?

Sure enough, during the first take after lunch, it starts right up again. Unbelievable, really, because we are all determined not to let Bryan down. This time, there's no farting, no craziness—just five five-year-olds trying desperately *not* to laugh during a funeral.

We fuck up the second half of the day as badly as we'd fucked up the first. Not on purpose, mind you. It just happened.

"Alright, that's a wrap," Bryan says a few hours later. "I'll figure out how to cut the fucking scene together later. Thanks for nothing, guys."

True to his word, Bryan figured out how to cut the fucking scene together. Boy, did he. To his credit, he pieced together a day's worth of outtakes featuring five idiots fucking around into something brilliant. He went into the editing room and crafted the scene beautifully, turning our dickish behavior into something that conveyed the screenplay's big "fuck you" to the cops. It was far more iconic than five guys just looking straight ahead and saying, "Give me the keys, you fucking cocksucker."

The reason the suspects have so much fun in front of the camera is that we have so much fun away from the camera. Getting to know Gabriel Byrne, for instance, is pretty great. That dark, brooding Irishman is one of the greatest so-called pussy magnets to make it to America, and there've been some killers, to be sure. (Sorry, Liam, ya can't touch him.) There's something about Gabriel that makes women think they can save him from his pain; he plays that tortured artist/poet role quite well, too. But he has a great sense of humor, and some of my fondest memories of the shoot involve Spacey and me trying to teach Gabriel how to impersonate Johnny Carson.

Heeeeere's Gabriel!

Postscript

That movie is the definition of lightning in a bottle. You want definitive proof? Look no further than Stephen Baldwin's really terrific performance.

You know where to find me, Stephen. Come and get me, tough guy. Bring Jesus.

(I'm kidding, Stephen. We both know you could beat my ass if need be. I'm happy for you that you found Jesus, actually. Let's face it, you can only snort an eight-ball off a hooker's back for so long.)

I remember when we first met on set. You came to work wearing leather pants.

Leather pants.

You hadn't arrived on a motorcycle. You were just wearing black leather pants.

Leather pants.

I don't know if you remember, but I looked at your leather pants and said, "Your brothers must've stolen your food at every meal, yeah?")

Post-Postscript

Kevin Spacey is a wonderful impressionist. He does a great Jack Lemmon and a wonderful Walter Matthau, not to mention a Christopher Walken that became famous thanks to a <u>Star Wars</u> auditions sketch on

But Enough about You . . . Eli Roth

It was the mid-nineties, and I remember coming home to my New York City apartment on 25th Street to find my roommate, Randy, watching late-night television. At first, I thought he was watching a Christopher Walken film, but then I quickly realized he was watching what was one of the most dead-on impressions that I had ever seen by any actor. Randy had a resemblance to a young Walken and often did a Walken impression as part of his stand-up act. We watched the television in awe.

Randy shook his head. "He's a genius. It's just too good."

I couldn't believe what I was seeing. "I had no idea Kevin Spacey did impressions."

He looked at me like I was a dog walking on its hind legs. "That's Kevin Pollak." And that's how I learned the difference.

Saturday Night Live. The bit is truly hilarious, but Spacey's Walken is so exaggerated that . . . well . . . it's actually pretty lame now, in my learned opinion.

His greatest impression, though, is one I don't think anyone has seen: William Hurt. It's genius, flawless, and spooky.

Post-Post-Postscript

There's a tale from the set of The Usual Suspects that trumps all the tales I've shared here. For that matter, it trumps any Hollywood tale you may have ever heard. And I mean any Hollywood tale. It took many smart people to convince me that I shouldn't share it in these pages. Having said that, if you see me in a bar some night, and you buy me just the right number of drinks, and you swear that if anybody asks, you didn't hear it from me, I'll tell ya.

30

The Suspects Go to Cannes

The American distribution for *The Usual Suspects* is completely botched. It opens in only three hundred theaters in the United States—a number that eventually grows to eight hundred—and yeah, it stars nobody so it's tough to market, but still. Only three hundred screens? Horrible.

To put those numbers in perspective, the year it opens domestically, 1995, a typical studio release is booked into two thousand theaters, so there's no way we'll be able to compete. We figure we're fucked, and we're right. It makes $22 million, which, in the grand scheme of things, is a monstrous disappointment.

Europe, however, is a different story.

The film debuts at the International Cannes Film Festival, and when Gabriel, Spacey, Benicio, Bryan, and I arrive at the festival, it's as total unknowns—OK, that's not exactly true, Gabriel was and still is pretty big in Europe—but, even a few days before that fateful screening, the crazed festival photogs celebrate our arrival as if we're box office gold.

At the premiere, the thousand photographers who line either side of the longest red carpet possible snap our pictures, and reporters fire off questions before they'd even had a chance to see the movie. (For that matter, other than Bryan, *we* hadn't seen the movie.)

But Enough about You . . . Adam Carolla

I had the opportunity to do Kevin's Ultra-net show in 2009, and three years later people are still buzzing about it, and by people I mean Kevin. But seriously, a lot of comics talk about the comedians that inspired them to do stand-up. After seeing Kevin's act, I'm seriously considering getting back into carpet cleaning.

The *Suspects* do Cannes: Benicio Del Toro, me, Gabriel Byrne, and Kevin Spacey, all jet-lagged as fuck. Despite our exhaustion, our first day of press for *The Usual Suspects* was exceptionally fun.

As we bound up the many, many steps to the grand theater, the photogs yell, "Gabriel! Gabriel! Gabriel!" Which is fine. I mean, he *is* the sexy one. (Benicio's hot now, but then nobody knows him from fucking Adam.)

Why the attention? Turns out the buzz stems from *Pulp Fiction* winning the Palme d'Or the year before. Since *Suspects* is in the same (what they're calling) gangster film family, expectations are riding high . . . and those expectations are met apparently because after the screening the audience gives us a really, really, *really* long standing ovation. It seems like it lasts twenty minutes. Granted, Cannes audiences are known for their lengthy bouts of applause, but it still feels remarkable, especially since the French have been known to boo filmmakers and actors out of that same theater. They can't wait to shit on you, but, boy, they also can't wait to love you.

There's a bunch of parties afterward, during one of which I run into Roger Ebert in, of all places, a buffet line. Roger had offered his review of *The Usual Suspects* earlier that day, and, while it wasn't a thumbs-down, it wasn't glowing, and he made a point of not predicting great things for its future, even after seeing the twenty-minute ovation.

"Hey, Rog, sorry you didn't like our movie. Guess the French didn't see the thing the same way you did."

"Yeah, yeah, yeah, I think I may have been tired."

"Have another roll," I say, pointing at his full plate, still feeling pissy about his crap review. "Or maybe a nap."

> Note: We've seen each other numerous times since, and he's always been quite friendly.

The Usual Suspects eventually rakes in over $100 million in its European theater run; it was so huge in Paris, in fact, that it played in one theater there for ninety-two consecutive weeks. Yes, almost *two years*. Its popularity created an international audience for all of us, and most importantly, it gave us all kinds of street cred in the indie world.

By the way, on that trip, Benicio got laid more than all of us put together. Just sayin'.

Postscript

As you'll recall, the budget for The Usual Suspects *was a little over $5 million, so we all are working for coffee and doughnuts, but we're confident that we'll make up for it on the back-end, specifically VHS and, many years later, DVD sales. We each got a net point, and a net point usually means nothing. (A net point is 1 percent of the producers' back-end participation after all the marketing and distribution expenses are recouped by the financiers.) In this case, since the movie cost $5 million* but it's made hundreds of millions, some have asked how it is that said single net point meant a little less than nothing.

There have been more <u>Suspects</u> "special DVD editions" than I can count, and the people who currently own the film's rights can rerelease it as many times as they want, so, if it keeps selling, why not? They don't need our permission for the releases themselves, but we need to sign off on the DVD extras—interviews, commentary, etc. At some point, Gabriel Byrne got tired of it.

In 2011, when yet another special DVD edition was being prepared, all the suspects received an e-mail asking for our permission to move forward. CC-ing everybody, Gabriel responded with something along the lines of, "I'm tired of taking it up the ass every sixteen fucking months just so somebody thinks they can fucking make another $50 million for the film that we fucking bled and sweated for, and we're still not seeing a fucking dime." He capped it off with a line from the film: "Forgive me, but you can all fuck yourselves."

God bless that wonderful man.

31

Sucking Face with Supermodels

Miami Rhapsody was a wonderful little film that starred Sarah Jessica Parker, Antonio Banderas, Mia Farrow, and, of course, me. It was notable for two firsts: my first onscreen kiss and my first experience with a method actor.

Let's start with the method madness.

When shooting on location—as was the case here, South Beach, Florida—actors often go out for meals as a group. When I'm part of these groups, I'm inevitably the class clown . . . which not many know is the agreement you sign when you're voted Class Clown in high school. Oh, yes, that's a fact.

As such, I take my clowning obligations and duties pretty seriously, so when the *Miami Rhapsody* cast goes out to dinner, I make certain the whole table is laughing at all times. There is one holdout, however— the actress playing my wife, a lovely woman named Barbara Garrick. Her reaction to all of my efforts is either an eye roll or a loud *tsk*.

I guess I'm just not her cup of tea, I think, but then I begin to notice this pervasive, almost pointed effort on her part to undermine my jokes, my happiness, my *everything*. It's so consistent that I began to wonder, *What the fuck is this woman's problem?*

Then it's brought to my attention: She's a method actress.

Oh, fuck . . .

See, in the movie, the husband I play cheats on his wife with a gorgeous model, portrayed by gorgeous *super*model Naomi Campbell. Barbara's character finds out about the cheating, so her character hates my character for almost the entire film. It becomes clear to me that since everyone else finds me funny *except her*, Barbara must've decided to hate me off camera because she doesn't want to let go of her on-camera hate—even for lunch.

Bullshit, I think. It's pretentious, and it doesn't take me long to decide that I hate method actors. Just do the fucking work when the cameras are on, but don't take it to the restaurant. Don't be a bitch to me because my character cheats on your character. Get over yourself. (That's about as raw and as honest as I'll ever be about an actor because I do believe in solidarity among actors. And thieves.)

I never confront Barbara because it's her process, and I don't want to mess with that. All that said, she was amazing in the film, period. Perhaps not surprisingly, she's far better and more believable than I am. In retrospect, it's more than possible that she was frustrated with me, the comedian with zero acting technique, trying so very hard to fit in with all the *real* actors off camera. It could also be that she found me and my jokes obnoxious, and her cold reaction to my class clowning had absolutely nothing to do with my talent deficiencies. If I judged you wrong all these years, Ms. Garrick, I'd like to think that I'm mature enough now to apologize for such awful things I chose to write about you in my book.

> I'd *like* to think that I'm mature enough to apologize. I'd also like to think that I'm taller and still have my thick, curly full head of hair from when we worked together. Ya know, when you were so cold to me on and off the set? Remember?

My first screen kiss is far more enjoyable.

It takes me fourteen movies to get that kiss—so long that they could've had me mash face with Roseanne Barr, and I would've been happy as hell. But instead, I get supermodel Naomi Campbell. (This is long before Naomi was spitting on and slapping policemen. She was just your everyday, run-of-the-mill supermodel.)

As excited as I was about the kiss, I was relieved that it was a funny moment. Unless there's something humorous attached to it, nobody wants to see me making out with Naomi Campbell . . . other than me, of course. For that matter, this scene is, as I write this, playing on all seven of the televisions throughout my home. On a continuous loop.

That's not true.

I only have five televisions.

The setup: Naomi's character is a model (quite a stretch there) married to my business partner, and during a dinner for the two couples, she mentions that she has a photo shoot on the beach the following day. I wonder aloud what that would be like, and she invites me to join her. The next afternoon, I go to the beach and knock on her trailer. When I go in, our eyes meet in the mirror, and we have That Moment. I move to kiss her, and she pushes me away. I apologize for making a move, and she explains that she can't kiss me because she has a bobby pin in her mouth. She removes the bobby pin and pulls me in. We kiss, ha, ha, ha, funny, terrific.

Now, when the comedian in me initially read the script, I know instinctively that for that moment to be as funny as it possibly can be, when I go in to kiss her, I have to really *get in there*, ya know? Tongues waggin' and everything. However, the moment that the comedian in me realizes this, the insecure Jew in me instantly decides that I could never suggest this to the director, David Frankel, for fear that he'll say, "Bullshit, you just want to tongue Naomi Campbell."

Well, *yeah.*

Weeks and weeks of shooting go by, and I don't say anything to David.

Finally, it's Kiss Day. I still haven't said anything to him, but it's killing me because I know that it won't be funny unless I get *in there*—but I can't say a word.

Before we shoot, we do a quick rehearsal; when the kiss moment comes along, it's just a little peck. *Fuck*, I think, *it's not gonna be funny*, but I just can't say anything to David.

"Alright, everybody, take your places!" he calls out a couple of minutes later. "We're gonna shoot this thing!" Then he strolls over to me. "Kevin, great rehearsal, really, great. It's just that, we're gonna *shoot* this now, and when it comes to the kiss, I think ya gotta . . . you know . . . you've gotta *get in there*. Give her a French kiss. It'll make it weird and funny—way funnier, don't ya think?"

"Listen, I'm a professional, and, if that's what works for you, I'm pretty sure I can do it. Of course, you may want to mention it to Naomi. I don't want her to slap me. Or vomit."

"Actually"—*beat, beat, beat*—"it was her idea."

I look David straight in the eyes and whisper: "I want that whore off the set."

Postscript

Right after we shoot the scene, I walk into the hair and makeup truck, and there's Naomi talking on her cell phone. "No, darling, I told you I have to kiss him . . . No, I'm just making out with him . . . a little . . . Come on, darling, you're an actor, you know what this is like . . . No, of course, I don't care for him. Please. It's just a long movie kiss."

Of the two of us, I thought I'd be the one discussing this kiss on the phone. Ya know, calling everyone I've ever met to tell them that I'm making out with NAOMI CAMPBELL. I never fathom that she would discuss this with anyone, ever in her life, let alone on the set.

Then it dawns on me: That's how you deal with a suspicious significant other.

Eventually, she hangs up the phone. I don't want to pry, but I'm dying to know what all the fuss is about. Naomi probably senses this because after a minute of awkward silence, she says, "That was my boyfriend. He's very jealous of you."

"Well, he needn't be because I'm sure whomever you're dating is Tom Terrific."

She smiles a smile that screams "You have no idea!" "Yes, but he doesn't like me kissing anyone."

"But you explained that it's just a movie . . ."

"Oh, he knows. He's kissed lots of women in movies. He knows it's nothing. Nothing. But he's being such an asshole."

"You know who her boyfriend is, don't you?" the hairdresser asks after she gets up and leaves.

"No. I'm sure someone fantastic, but I don't read the tabloids, so I haven't a clue, no."

"It's Robert De Niro," he whispers.

Cool. Robert De Niro wants me dead. Life doesn't get any better, does it?

Post-Postscript

It's worth mentioning here that when I kissed Daryl Hannah on <u>Grumpy Old Men</u>, I had to stand on an apple box so I could reach her lips. Also worth mentioning: her boyfriend at the time was John F. Kennedy Jr., and he came to visit the set on the day she and I were shooting our kiss.

Curious . . . or jealous?

When he walked unannounced into the hair and makeup truck to see her, having just arrived from out of town, I melted into the chair. His presence carried the entire family history with it, and his smile was so incandescent I swear he was signaling somebody on the moon.

But Enough about You . . . James Roday

Let's be honest: KP is an easy target. He was one of the androgynous nymphs in *Willow,* and I'm almost positive he's Samm Levine's father. Look, I'm not trying to beat him around and drain him of what little dignity he still carries in his little manpurse that he got as a gift from the crew of *Miami Rhapsody.* I'm taking the high road because I've actually seen Kevin at his best, and all twelve of you should hear about it.

I met KP in 2001 in Austin, Texas. Together we participated in an experience I will never forget. On the heels of one of the gravest days our country had ever experienced, we were filming a comedy about a quintet of misfits who travel from Texas to Kansas in hopes of harvesting the US government's largest marijuana forest. Overcome with grief and the horrors of our new reality, many of us questioned whether we were doing the right thing—or if, in fact, we even *could* deliver funny under the circumstances.

Our esteemed director had cashed in a number of favors in hope of surrounding his cast of unknowns (including myself) with as many colorful cameos as possible. One by one, phone call by phone call, they all pulled out. Nobody wanted to get on a plane, and who could possibly blame them? Not to mention the very strong possibility that they were all struggling with the same questions we were.

Except for Kevin Pollak. He showed up. With all the same concerns but somehow mitigating them enough to get on a plane, fly to Texas, and support a friend who'd been given an opportunity to do something he'd never done before. I'll never forget that. In some small way, the act of showing up transcended the philosophical, spiritual, and moral conundrum of our situation and validated the very reason that it was OK for us to be there. People needed to laugh. Everywhere.

Granted, we could only guarantee that the skeleton crew of *Rolling Kansas* would be giggling every day of that shoot, but that was something. That was *anything*. I'm not sure if we, as Americans, have ever looked to find ourselves in others the way we did in the wake of 9/11. Certainly not in my lifetime. Kevin Pollak showed up. And he was awesome and treated all of us greenies with respect and true aplomb.

I've said this before, and I'll say it again—I'm quite certain that I'll never have another experience like I had working on that film. It was catharsis, a rite of passage, and a chance to watch KP soak through a wool suit and wipe most of his head with a handkerchief so many times that I stopped counting. Most of all, it's a source of pride. I truly hope KP feels the same way. We've never really spoken of it because he's a petty bastard, and that wasn't a money job.

I wonder if he even remembers doing it.

Shit.

32

Nixon's List

Canadian Bacon, Michael Moore's only foray into fictional filmmaking, had one helluva cast: the marvelous Alan Alda, the hilarious John Candy (in his final film), the spunky Rhea Perlman, the wonderful character actor Kevin J. O'Connor, and the truly insane Rip Torn.

I'd been a Rip fan since his oddly funny performance in Albert Brooks's *Defending Your Life* and then on Garry Shandling's *The Larry Sanders Show*. At that point, one and all acknowledged him as pretty hilarious. One and all also acknowledged him as pretty eccentric, although this is news to me. I could guess by his work that he wasn't at all normal; he never seemed comfortable in his own skin while acting in a scene. It just didn't seem like an acting choice but rather a man behaving oddly because that was normal to him.

And I was right.

I just didn't know to what degree.

Some backstory on Rip: Originally he was supposed to play the Jack Nicholson role in *Easy Rider*, the role that skyrocketed Jack to fame. Rip, apparently, considered himself more talented than Nicholson, and word on the street was that he never got over it. Garry Shandling was so concerned about Rip's mental state—and how it might wreak havoc on a set if he cast him in *Larry Sanders*—that he called up his friend Albert Brooks, who had reinvented Rip's career by casting him in *Defending Your Life*.

"I'm about to hire Rip Torn for my TV show," Shandling said, "and I was wondering if you could clarify my growing concern."

"Garry, buddy, you know I love you," Albert said, and I'm paraphrasing here, "so I don't know if I would wish this upon you. But if you can get him to focus and stay in the groove, he's brilliant beyond your wildest dreams. But yes, he can be a little bit of trouble."

As the story goes, Garry went to Rip and said, "OK, I've heard you can cause trouble on the set. This is a great part, and you'd be great in it. But I've done a television show before, and my life is too short to have problems on the set. I want everyone on the crew and cast to enjoy this job, ya know? If you can promise me that you won't be a problem to work with, I would love you to play this part, and I would be honored to have you on the show. But I really need you to look inside yourself because, if you say you're fine and we start shooting and you're not, well, I would rather cancel the show than do five years with a crazy person."

Again, I'm paraphrasing.

"I've had my troubles, but it's all behind me," Rip allegedly said. "I'll be there for you, Garry. Don't worry."

Then he proceeded to be a nightmare for six seasons—but he was so great in the part that there was nothing Garry could do.

I can't imagine what it was like to do six seasons with Rip because one movie was more than enough for me. I mean, this guy shut down production every single day we shot.

Every. Single. Day.

It's like he carried a black cloud of negativity everywhere he went. There was always a sense of danger, like he'd explode any second. John Belushi made that sense of danger funny; with Rip Torn, it's horrifying.

Rip's paranoid rants are mind-blowing. Most every day, he goes off either on a member of the cast or the crew who he believes is out to get him, and every day, every time, it's somebody different; then he goes into a corner and sulks and tells anybody who will listen that, "I'm not gonna go on the set until [fill in the blank] is removed or apologizes." Of course, the target du jour had *never* done anything wrong.

One of his standard tirades was about President Richard Nixon. If I heard Rip roar, "*I was on Nixon's list!*" once, I heard it a thousand times. (I had no idea Nixon even had a list.) But it doesn't end there. "Nixon tracked me down to these Communist meetings. I was twenty, and everybody was going to those things. If you wanted to get laid, you went to the meetings."

I have to admit, though, it's hilarious. Frightening as anything I'd ever witnessed, granted, but hilarious.

> The majority of his bad behavior went down after our lunch break. As you read the phrase "lunch break," I ask you to imagine me extending my thumb and pinky to make the international gesture for "drinky-drinky."

For some reason, Rip considers me a fellow conspirator and likes to confide in me about who's out to get him. Still, I figure it's only a matter of time before he turns on me. But when he does, it's still shocking because, until that moment, we were really friendly. Dare I say it, we had a kinship.

He's reading off-camera lines for me, and he keeps fucking up; after far too many takes, it becomes obvious that this is another cry for attention. Why would a veteran actor like Rip Torn fuck up his off-camera work, time after time after time? Michael Moore and I later figure it was because, during this conversation scene between Rip and me, Michael shot my coverage first.

After the sixteenth fuckup, I ask him, "Do you want to hold the sides?"—film-speak for a shrunken version of the script that you can hold in your hand. "If it'll help to hold the sides while you're off camera and read them if you need to, that's fine by me."

BOOM!

"Michael, I need a minute," he says and storms off set. Everyone looks at one another, wondering what could've gone wrong or upset him.

The first assistant director tells everyone to take five, so I head over to the craft service table to grab some coffee. By the time I return, Michael is sitting in front of the video monitors, watching the scene he filmed while the shit hit the fan.

"It's your turn, I guess," he says to me. "Rip said, 'You and Kevin Pollak don't tell me what to do . . . I've been in this business for fifty fucking years . . . before you were born . . . That guy telling me to read . . . I don't need to hold the goddamned script, little son of a bitch . . . I'm not coming back until Kevin Pollak is removed from the set!'

"I told him, 'I'm not removing Kevin, Rip. We're not done shooting the scene, and if you want us to shoot the scene without your coverage, fine. You just stay right over here. I'm gonna go back and finish my movie.'"

When you have people this crazy on your set, people start to joke about them as a way to relieve the tension. It's human nature. One afternoon, Kevin J. O'Connor pulls a few of us aside and tells us that he and his new bride are staying in the hotel room next to Rip's. (We're all staying at the Four Seasons in Toronto, but lucky Kevin J. and Mrs. Kevin J. share a wall with Rip.)

"I don't have physical evidence of this," Kevin J. continues, "but, well, we can hear him yelling at a woman every night, and we started to notice that it isn't the same woman. We also started to notice that the things he's yelling at these women . . . well, it dawns on us that these women are strangers . . . whom he had, shall we say, rented for the evening. And the stuff he's yelling at these women is so horrifying and disgusting in a sexual nature that it's become hilarious to my wife and me. It got so disturbing that we thought we had to do something to get through feeling horrible for these women. We decided to put together a top ten list of The Things Rip Torn Yelled at the Hookers from the Other Side of the Wall."

The first nine have been lost to the sands of time, but I will never forget the Number One Thing Rip Torn Yelled at the Hookers from the Other Side of the Wall:

(drumroll please)

"I said . . . MILK IT LIKE A COW!"

Postscript

Fifteen years later, I run into Kevin J. O'Connor for the first time since <u>Canadian Bacon</u>.

"Kevin, I have to tell you something," I say. "I've been dining on the 'milk it like a cow' story for fifteen years. But it's been a long time, and I'm wondering if I've made something more out of it than it was."

"Tell me the story the way you've been telling everybody else."

I give him the dissertation I've just given to you, dear reader, after which he smiles. "Yes, that's exactly what happened."

33

The Don

Sometimes the sheer boredom of being an actor on a film set can undermine even the greatest acting opportunities. For me, there was no greater instance of this than on the set of *Casino*.

Bob Richardson is a multi-Academy-Award-winning cinematographer, and, when you combine his genius with Martin Scorsese's well-documented attention to detail, you're looking at the potential, dare I say, the likelihood, of an average wait time between most setups of between at least one and two hours.

Before I continue, let me be clear: This is in no way an effort on my part to complain. In fact, let's be *damn* clear. Although actors work, on average, twelve hours a day while on a film, we spend eleven of those twelve hours sitting on our asses either on the set or in a trailer. Honestly, I'm not even sure it's a job, per se.

Having said all that, the sheer joy of watching Don Rickles go after Robert De Niro offsets the often-endless waiting game on the set of *Casino*. I've improvised onstage with the likes of Robin Williams, but I've never seen anybody make up material faster than Don Rickles did on the set of *Casino*.

Two particularly tremendous moments:

One: We're shooting a scene on the casino floor in which Don, looking like a disgruntled manservant, stands next to De Niro and discusses a problem he's having with Pesci's character.

> I actually get buddy-buddy enough with Rickles to suggest his style of acting in *Casino* only involved looking old and disgruntled. Rickles, who needs little to no instigating to work himself into a lather, retaliates.

Yeah, the band's name is bigger, but I have a better font.

"Hey, kid, listen, I saw your name on the marquee down the street"—my stand-up agent thought that, since I was in Las Vegas for twenty weeks, it would be a heads-up ball to get me a gig at one of the casinos—"and, boy oh boy, opening up for the *Four Tops*. That's exciting, yeah. Ya know, I'm gonna be on tour with Sinatra in a couple of months. You want tickets?"

Now you have to understand that, whenever De Niro walks onto the set, everyone whispers, "There he is, there *he is*," after which every sphincter tightens shut. The rest of us will never see this level of respect.

Rickles, however, is not impressed.

Marty calls, "Action," and De Niro begins the scene; one minute in—right in the middle of the shot, with the great De Niro speaking his lines—Rickles breaks character and turns to De Niro. "Is that the way you're gonna do it? Like *that*?"

De Niro makes a face that says, *Excuse me?*

"No, no, you got the awards. I'm sure you know what you're doing. Go ahead."

When Rickles launches into his shtick, the aforementioned sphincters tighten even more, and everybody lets out a collective gasp of *Oh shit*. Then: dead silence as everybody waits for De Niro's response.

Within seconds, thankfully, we get the now-famous laughing De Niro face, not dissimilar to the downturned gapped-mouth Tragedy frown attached to the upturned gapped-mouth Comedy smile. His upturned gapped mouth causes all to gap our own mouths. Turns out De Niro loves when Rickles rips into him.

Just like he said he would back in the lobby of the Bel-Air Hotel, Rickles *owns* De Niro.

Two: We're scheduled to shoot a news conference scene in which Alan King hands me a giant mock-up of a check for $67 million to fund the construction of a new hotel, The Tangiers. I arrive on set, and there are Alan, Rickles, and fifty extras portraying the journalists there to capture this moment in Las Vegas history. Don, Alan, and I sit at a table on the stage at the front of the room and wait for De Niro.

A *Casino* wedding. Why my character was at the wedding makes no sense, but if that's what Marty wants, that's what Marty gets. . . .

When Rickles notices the microphones on the table, he leans into one and proceeds to tear into all fifty of those hapless extras. "You're all extras, huh? What do you make, $30 a day and some bad fish off the truck? Good for you."

He rails for twenty minutes on what it's like to be an extra, twenty minutes of hilarious material that has these extras laughing themselves sick. He's having his way with them, and they cannot be happier.

Don runs himself ragged and sits back in his chair to rest. Thirty seconds of dead silence pass, then De Niro arrives. The moment Rickles sees De Niro, he lunges back at the microphone, and points at De Niro. "Alright, which one of you said he's *gay*? He's here now, say it to his *face*."

De Niro comes to a screeching halt, stares at Don, then makes that same gapped-mouth smile, and laughs until he can't breathe.

This goes on all day. We do a take, Marty yells, "Cut," then Rickles does ten minutes on De Niro. Again and again, everybody loves it. Who wouldn't love being insulted by Don Rickles?

Joe Pesci, that's who.

Joe doesn't like when Don turns his razor-sharp tongue on him. Pesci does not appreciate when, in front of two hundred extras, Rickles says, "Joe, you're so short, I'm gonna ride you around the set like a Shetland pony."

Pesci growls—yeah, that's right, *growls*—then says, "Oh, yeah, you're a fucking riot, Rickles. No, no, I get it, I get it—I'm a midget, and you're a *genius*. Go fuck yourself!" He wasn't interested in playing comedy tennis.

De Niro puts his hand on Pesci's shoulder. "Come on, Joe, don't—"

"Nah, fuck him with that."

Later, I see Joe walking back to his trailer, mumbling to himself. "Fucking Rickles, that prick. Motherfucker. *Fuck* him."

"Hey, Joe, come on," I say. "He was just kidding around."

"Yeah, you're *another* one," he roars. "The two-a-ya's, go fuck yourselves."

When he wasn't all wound up, Joe was engaging, funny, and fun to hang out with on set. But when The Don got under his skin, forget it.

34

Have You Seen the Muffin, Man

Before we shoot *Casino*, Marty Scorsese tells me that my character, Phillip Green, is based on a gentleman who's still alive. "You may want to meet him at some point, but we're not sure he wants to participate. But if that's something you want, we'll try and arrange it."

"Well, my research is in the script," I say. "That's how I work."

In typical Marty fashion, he launches into a twenty-minute tangent about the genius of Nick Pileggi's script, the importance of preparation, and the joy of working with actors with a great work ethic—a tangent that could have been delivered in four words: "That's a good idea."

> This isn't to say that Marty's tangents are bad. Actually, they make me feel as if I'm attending a Mensa class about filmmaking. I just have no idea how he ever gets any work done with his predilection for telling the greatest—and longest—stories ever heard about the history of film.

Phillip Green isn't a big part—ultimately onscreen for about nine minutes of the film's almost-three-hours—but since Marty is Marty, I need to be available for the whole twenty-week shoot. That's five months on set for nine minutes on screen.

"Marty's the kind of guy," my agent explains, "who'll wake up and say he wants to shoot this instead of that, so they've learned to keep everybody around. But whenever they can figure out a time for you to take a three- or four-day break, they'll cut you loose and let you go back home."

I'm not thrilled about this arrangement, but I love gambling, so all in all it's not bad. Not bad at all.

All the casino scenes are shot at the shithole Riviera, which, shockingly enough, is still there on the strip, looking exactly like it did in 1994, which was exactly how it looked in 1974. The producers make a deal with the hotel so everybody can have suites . . . except for Marty, De Niro, Sharon Stone, and Joe, who are staying somewhere considerably, considerably fancier. Considerably.

The Riviera suites are humongous and fantastic in size. But the decor was tired when the hotel opened, and by the time I get there, I can't even stand to look at it. Which is just as well, actually, because I spend most of my time hanging out in the casino or with Don Rickles.

I'm only in one scene alone with De Niro—the moment when he complains that my blueberry muffin has more blueberries than his— and before we shoot it I think, *Kevin, this is your opportunity to go toe-to-toe with one of the greatest actors of the last fifty years. Sure, there's no real emotion for you in the scene, but you have a chance to be believable. You also have a chance not to cry due to abject fear.*

Marty doesn't tell me what to do—and not just with me, with everybody. All he says is, "Alright, let's just get going and see what happens."

We do the scene, and it goes well. After it's done, there's a little bobbing head right at the end of the table.

It's Marty.

He'd crouched down to watch us, which surprises me because I didn't know he could get any closer to the ground than he is when he stands.

"That was great, just great, really, really, really great," he says. "So what do you think, Bob? More angry about the muffin? Less angry about the muffin?" Then, before De Niro can answer, to me: "What do you think, Kevin? Should your guy be more offended? Less offended?" Etc., etc.

After discussing it for a bit, we shoot another take. And another. And another. And another.

On the set of *Casino,* moody lighting courtesy of Academy Award–winner Bob Richardson. The intense, dramatic look in my eyes is not boredom from this being take #34, I swear.

The most important thing I learn that day is that Scorsese and De Niro like to do about thirty-five takes for every fucking setup—and I add the word "fucking" because I like to do about three takes for every fucking setup because after three takes I become aware of myself acting, and then that's all I'm thinking about instead of just being in the moment as the character.

De Niro, however, isn't concerned about that. He wants to try it thirty-five different ways. By the fifteenth take, I wonder, *Does he really not know how he wants to do this? Is he trying anything and everything because he can't find it?* I don't question his motives aloud—because I know that, between the two of us, he's the expert. Plus I want so very much to believe that takes four through thirty-five weren't a total waste of time.

There are so many takes that it starts to feel like we're speaking Spanish. I don't know what the words mean, I don't know who I am, I don't know who he's supposed to be, I don't know who anybody is. I look at De Niro and Marty, and think, *Why would anybody let you two maniacs make a movie?—because clearly there's not a moment of thought regarding budget or schedule.* It dawns on me that this is what greatness looks like when allowed to flourish unconditionally, so I try to figure out if I'm missing something by doing three takes, rather than thirty-five.

I try, I try, O Lord, I try.

But I do learn three things during the blueberry muffin day:

1. It's possible to do something slightly different every single take, regardless of how many takes there may be. If you truly focus, you can make every shot fresh and new.

2. Never, ever be satisfied with what you've done until Marty says, "I think we've got it."

3. Dread the question "What do you think, should we do one more?"

This was one of the few days on *Casino* when "Bob" spoke to me. He made a crack about the size of my bow tie. Fuck him.

Postscript

On the set, most everybody calls De Niro "Bob"—but not me. I don't think I referred to him by his name for the entire shoot. I never felt like I could go right up to him and say, "Hey, Bob, how's tricks?" He never seemed real to me. I felt more uncomfortable around him than any other human being in my life. I'd like to think that has to do with the fact that he's super-duper focused on his work. The rare times that he shot the shit, it felt like God was taking a cigarette break and I was the only one nearby.

35

Club Willis

If I hadn't met Bruce Willis when shooting *A Few Good Men*, and if I hadn't met Matthew Perry while visiting Courteney Cox on the set of *Friends*, I would never have been able to play a Hungarian-born, Chicago-raised hitman named Janni Gogolak in *The Whole Nine Yards*. I say that because, when my name is floated to director Jonathan Lynn, he says, "Fellas, I'm a fan of Kevin Pollak. I've seen *The Usual Suspects*, and I've seen *A Few Good Men*, and he's very diverse, but this is a *comedy*."

That's how strong a left-turn my career had taken, that an established comedy director didn't know I was a stand-up comedian or that I could even be funny in a film. That old saying became crystal clear: "Be careful what you wish for." Since I had street cred as a dramatic actor, I wasn't allowed to do comedy.

> I'm always open to tackle any genre, and this is something all young actors or comics should know: If you don't diversify, you won't survive unless you reach the very top, and that just doesn't happen too often. Diversify, work your ass off, and keep open to zigging and zagging.

Anyhow, Bruce and Matthew convince Jonathan that I can be funny, so I'm hired. Before we began shooting, I say to the director, "According to the script, Janni is Hungarian-born and Chicago-raised. Which accent do you want?"

"Can you give me both? At the same time?"

I hadn't thought of that. I give him hard Chicago consonants and the Hungarian V and W flip-flop. Example: "My fadder vas a great man, a man of wision and character."

Doing the accent: fun. Shooting the film in Montreal: fun. Club Willis at the InterContinental Hotel: *Big* fun.

They'd been shooting for over a week when I show up on set for my first day. While I'm in the makeup and hair trailer, Matthew sidles over. "You coming to Club Willis tonight?"

"Where?"

"Oh, you're gonna love this. After you finish work tonight, you go back to the hotel, you go up to the penthouse floor, you get out of the elevator, and you're at Club Willis. It's more than just that, though. You'll see."

"Can you tell me any more?"

"Nope."

We finish shooting, I go back to the hotel, I shower, I go up to the penthouse floor, I exit the elevator, and I discover what it must have been like to party with Elvis.

Bruce has the entire penthouse floor to himself. When I get off the elevator, I'm in a giant foyer that leads to an even more giant living room. All the furniture in the living room has been removed save for the couches and end tables flush up against every wall, creating a dance floor in the middle. On the ceiling, in the dead center of the makeshift dance floor hangs a mirror ball. Somebody had procured and set up a sound system fit for a stadium, and no one complained about the volume being too low. There's even a bar with a bartender.

Holy shit.

Bruce was still showering, and Matthew is the only other person in the room, so he comes over. "What're you drinking?"

"Uhhhhhhhh, I don't know." I point at his glass. "What're you drinking?"

"Vodka."

"Good. Vodka." After he gets me a drink, I ask, "So how does this work, Matthew? What the fuck is going on?"

He smiles. "Just wait."

Over the next hour, more people drift into the room; they get some drinks and sit down on the sofas. Everybody has one thing in common: They're all dudes. Eventually, Bruce appears.

"Scotty, gimme a six," he tells the bartender, which, I later find out, means he wants six fingers of vodka in a glass with a couple of ice cubes.

Not too long after, a couple of guys from Bruce's inner circle show up with seven women in their mid-twenties. These women take to the empty dance floor, and within thirty seconds it's *on*. They're ridiculously talented, ridiculously attractive strippers imported from the town's finest venues. It's the cream of the crop. And they're dancing. On the dance floor. Under the disco ball. So the fellas can watch. These ladies aren't messing around. They are, in fact, actually competing for our attention.

I'm married at the time, and, even though I'm one of the few men at the party not hitting on the girls, it's the most amazing Felliniesque show.

Funniest moment: Our costar, Michael Clarke Duncan, walks into the room and, without saying a word to anybody, grabs one of the girls by the hand, and says in that deep, booming voice of his: "Let's go." Which she gladly did.

That was my introduction to Club Willis, a club open only to us, where the booze was flowing in numbered sizes and where you could find the best talent in town every night of the week.

Postscript (or possibly a prescript) (or maybe even a side-script)

When I first met Matthew Perry and mentioned to him that I was trying to develop a television show, he told me, "I'm an insane fan. I can literally recite every line from A Few Good Men. Why would you want to develop a TV show? You're an amazing film actor."

"The grass is always greener, pal."

"Are you not thrilled to death with your particular place in the sun? Anybody in the Friends cast would kill to do what you're doing."

"And I would kill to do what you're doing. Let's face it, starring in a smash sitcom is the single greatest job in showbiz."

He knew I was right, as does anyone who works on a multiple-camera, taped-in-front-of-a-live-audience sitcom.

Let me break down the hours for you—because they're fantastic: Monday, you show up to a table read at 11:00. You do your read, then you go home; at most, you're there for an hour. Tuesday, you rehearse from 10:00 to 3:00 with a huge lunch break. Wednesday, 10:00 to 3:00 again, then a run-through for the network people at 3:30, with yet another huge lunch break. Thursday is the only difficult day. You show up at 9:00 (oh my God!), and you work until 5:00 or 6:00 (holy shit!), and the day is so long because every scene is camera blocked to the nth degree. Friday, the day you shoot the show, you show up at 1:00, you do a run-through at 3:00, you film in front of the audience at 6:00, and you're on your way home at 9:00. Not only that, you get every fourth week off. Not only that, you only work from August to March.

By the way, Matthew wasn't lying about one thing. While filming The Whole Nine Yards, while I was standing around on set waiting to do a scene, often in conversation with someone, he liked to sneak up behind me and recite a line of dialogue from A Few Good Men. And not the famous stuff—"You can't handle the blah blah blah"—no, I'm talking the most obscure lines in the film.

Funny every time.

But Enough about You . . . Matthew Perry

When I was first contacted by Kevin Pollak about writing something about him in a book he was writing about himself, my reaction was twofold: Firstly, I thought *Finally, there is someone more narcissistic than I am.* My second thought was, *How can I make this more about me than him?*

I grew up in Canada. My first loves were hockey and the movies. I am six feet tall and have blue eyes. I became wildly famous in 1994. I am a very good tennis player. My favorite movie is *Groundhog Day*. I have an infinity pool that looks out over the entire city. I am kind, honest, and get along beautifully with children. I am left of center politically but remain open to all ideas. I think world peace is a darn good thing. I don't dance often, but when I do dance, I mean it. I really mean it. Kevin Pollak was good in the movie *A Few Good Men*. I weigh 175 pounds. I've recently taken to going to the gym and as a result am beginning to see definition in my upper torso. My favorite song is "Here Comes the Sun" because I believe it is unapologetically hopeful and upbeat. Kevin Pollak was born on October 30, 1957. Here is a poem I have written about myself:

> *Roses are red.*
> *Violets are blue.*
> *Matthew Perry is a Leo*
> *who has definition in his upper torso.*

Now I would like you, reader, to put the book down and pause and think about me for a few moments.

Back? You're welcome.

Some quick notes on a scorecard, if you will, about me: I'm forty-two. My favorite color is blue. I enjoy playing beach volleyball. I have four sisters and one brother. My first acting job was on Scott Baio's *Charles in Charge*. Kevin Pollak plays poker.

36

Carpe Per Diem

If anybody cares, I can explain why successful actors often behave like children and/or crybabies and/or spoiled brats: It's because we're treated like six-year-olds who live with our parents.

When filming on location, we have our own room, and we don't have to do any cleaning or cooking. We're picked up and dropped off as if going to elementary school. We're fed a nice breakfast of pancakes or waffles or even cupcakes if that's what our little hearts desire. We're given a nice, long break for lunch. We're covered with costumes and makeup, so we can play dress-up and make-believe. Anytime during the day, if we need anything—a snack, iPads, sunglasses, three-toed sloths, whatever—all we need to do is raise our little hands, and somebody will run off and get it for us. Oh, and we're paid ridiculous sums of money, which makes us feel extra-special. Plus, when filming on location, we're given an allowance to spend as we wish, which grown-ups call per diem.

Per diems can run anywhere from $100 to $5,000 a day. (The irony is that folks making $20 million for a movie are possibly also raking in another $20,000 per week of per diem money. The more you have, the more you get.) But here's the thing: Our hotel rooms are paid for, our meals are paid for, and our transportation is paid for. Per diem is responsibility-free cash-money, and it's just another great perk on top of all the other great perks.

Even though per diem is Latin for "for the day," we get our allowance once a week, and every week it's the same drill: On a given day, a production assistant arrives on set and hands out cash envelopes to everybody, for which we sign. On *The Whole Nine Yards*, each of us receives our envelope every Thursday. One Thursday night, about halfway through the shoot, there's a knock at my trailer door, followed by a cry of "Mr. Pollak, they're ready for you!" I open the door, and there's a P.A. standing next to the teamster-driven van that will make the three-minute drive to the set. Before I get into the van, the P.A. hands me an envelope and says, "Please sign for your per diem, Mr. Pollak."

As I'm signing, from behind me, the insanely low-registered voice of Michael Clarke Duncan says, "Where's my per diem?"

I turn around. "Hey, Mike."

Michael is 6'3" tall and five feet wide. I'm 5'6" tall and no feet wide.

The P.A. instantly turns into the pimply, cracked-voice character from *The Simpsons*. "Sorry, M-m-m-m-mister D-d-d-d-uncan. I d-d-d-don't know what h-h-h-h-h-h-happened to your per diem."

"What the hell you sayin', 'you don't know what happened to my per diem'? How come he signin' for his per diem, and you didn't bring me mine."

"I-I-I-I'm just handing out w-w-w-w-what they gave me, M-m-m-m-mister D-d-d-d-uncan."

Michael points to my envelope. "How do I know that's not *my* per diem he's signin' for right there? That could me *mine* right there, is what I'm sayin'."

I'm laughing because I'm sure that Michael's fucking with the P.A. But his lack of a smile squelches my laughter. You could say his expression was menacing. To say the least.

"Well, s-s-s-s-sir, you could s-s-s-s-see that right there on the envelope, it s-s-s-s-says 'Kevin Pollak.' That's the only r-r-r-r-reason I'm giving it to him, s-s-s-s-sir."

"Well, why don't you make that my per diem, then you could go back and get his."

"Mike," I say, making sure to have a big smile on my face, "look what it says on the envelope. It's got my name on it. Let the kid go back to the office and get your per diem. What's the big deal? Come on."

He lets it go, and we pile in the van to drive to the set. When we arrive, I head over to Bruce and Matthew, who are happily relaxing in their chairs. You can tell they're their chairs because they have their names on the back. In fact, that's how you can tell who some of your co-stars are when you're not working with people as famous as Matthew and Bruce. We kibitz for forty-ish minutes, which is way too long to have Bruce Willis sitting around not acting.

And now a lengthy aside about how to treat big stars on the set.

The protocol on a movie shoot is that you call the star to the set when you're *ready* and not when you *think* you're ready. If you need to have them in front of the camera at exactly 11:58, you get them there at as close to 11:56 as humanly possible. It's one of the first assistant director's jobs to gauge exactly how long it takes each actor or actress to get from his or her respective trailer to the set once told, "They're ready for you now."

It's quite a delicate balancing act when you need, say, six of your actors on set to start a shot at the same time because potentially you're looking at six completely different concepts of time and space. Let's say, for example that you're the first A.D. and you know that the star—as in *number one on the call sheet*—takes about ten minutes after being invited to the set actually to leave the trailer and head to the set. You also know that the number four on the call sheet takes half a fucking hour, and number two takes, on average, seventeen minutes.

Turns out they don't ask those stupid logic questions on the SATs for nothing, kids. The best A.D.s are judged on this ability almost more than any other.

Another not-quite-as-lengthy aside about how to treat big stars on the set: I knew Tom Cruise was one of the most professional actors with whom I'd ever work when I saw how long it took him to leave his trailer for set. He literally bolted from the door within seconds of hearing, "We're ready, Tom," and I'm not exaggerating. It was as if he was in his trailer, constantly in a runner's crouch, waiting for the starter's pistol to fire.

One day early in the *Few Good Men* shoot, I'm walking back to set, and I see Tom running past me.

"Where's the fire, pal?" I say.

To which he responds, without breaking stride, "Come on, buddy. Shake a leg." Damn if that fucker didn't have me running to catch up.

So after those forty long minutes, Bruce turns to his longtime assistant, Stephen Eads. "What the fuck, Stevie?"

"Yeah," Stephen says, "I was wondering the same thing," then turns to a nearby P.A. "What the fuck?"

The P.A. runs off to find out what the fuck, then runs back and whispers something to Stephen, who then turns to me, Bruce, and Matthew. "There's a problem."

"What's the fucking problem?" we all say in unison.

"Uhhh, we're not sure. The crew has been ready to go for about thirty minutes, but apparently . . . something *weird* is going on, and nobody's saying what it is."

"That's not a real fucking answer," Bruce says. "Please go to set and find out what the fuck we're waiting on."

Stephen strolls off, then returns with Jonathan Lynn, our director, in tow.

"Um, right," Jonathan says in his British accent, "here's the thing, fellas—and Kevin, in particular—apparently Michael's refusing to work because you took his per diem."

I, of course, start laughing.

"Are you insane?" says Matthew. "Why would you take *his* per diem? He's a giant, ya know."

Still laughing, I tell the guys what happened back at the trailer. "So you see, I didn't take anybody's per diem."

As Bruce and Matthew crack up, Jonathan—who isn't cracking up—says, "Right. Hilarious. But. We can't go back to work until this is resolved."

"You know how this is gonna get resolved?" Bruce says. "I'm gonna fucking set him on fire."

"No, no," I say, "you know what? I'm happy to apologize to him for any misunderstanding and give him my per diem. I couldn't care less, really. If he wants to play crazy guy, let him play crazy guy. I just want to get the fuck back to work."

"Not. On. My. Fucking. Life." Bruce says. "You can forget about that. You're not giving him your fucking per diem."

"Bruce, let me go talk to him. Only he, I, and that unlucky P.A. know what really went down." I turn to Jonathan. "I don't know what stories he's been telling you, but he knows and I know that nobody stole anybody's per diem. Let me go over there and talk to him, man to man."

Jonathan asks Bruce if, for the sake of finishing this evening's shoot, we can proceed with the plan. Bruce says OK, so I walk over to Michael, who's sitting *way* on the other side of the set. The second he sees me, he turns away.

This is gonna be fun.

"Hey, Mike, listen, there's been a misunderstanding. I hear that you're upset, and I want you to know that I'm truly sorry if I was part of the reason you're upset. Maybe I should've let you and the P.A. work it out between the two of you."

He looks me in the eye—like only a truly crazy person can, and I know this for a fact because I'd previously stared crazy in the eye (I'm talking to you, Rip Torn)—and says, "Y'oughta think twice before takin' a man's per diem."

Oh. OK. So now he's convinced himself that his lie is the truth, and he's saying this to the only person on the set, other than himself, who knows his truth is a lie. But he's clearly upset (not to mention crazy), so I take the high road, partly because I'm a team-first kind of guy and partly because the low road is starting to freak me out.

"You're right. It seems I took your per diem. Not sure what I was thinking. It's back in my trailer, and I'll have a P.A. bring it to you, pronto. Sorry for the misunderstanding."

"Yeah," he sniffs, after which I walk away and go back to work.

The scene we're shooting that night featured Michael's character, Frankie Figs, pouring gas on me and my car so he can set us on fire. For the filming of this scene, Michael pours water out of the gas can and not real gas—as he may have preferred. To nobody's surprise, he empties the water onto me with such force and velocity that it feels as if I'm being water-boarded. It takes an unbelievable level of focus (A) not to break character and yell at him, or (B) to start weeping like a little girl.

As I towel off my face, I think, *Should I mention this to Bruce? No, probably not because he'll have the loon taken out back and shot. Better to let the idiot work it out of his system because this will all be over soon enough.*

Postscript

A couple of years later, I'm on a beach in Hawaii, thinking about the old working actor's adage, If you haven't worked in a while and you want a job, book a vacation. Sure as shit, keeping said adage alive, my cell rings, and it's Bruce Willis. As you can imagine, Bruce doesn't call that often, so I decide momentarily to set aside my foolish desire for sun and fun and answer the damn call.

"We're doing a sequel to The Whole Nine Yards," he says. "It'll be called The Whole Ten Yards. Sound good?"

"Well, Bruce, I'm sure you remember this: You shot and killed my character in The Whole Nine Yards. Are you calling to rub it in?"

Like I said, Ain't no money like sequel money.

We had to shoot *The Whole Ten Yards* on Super Bowl Sunday, and Matthew Perry and I have bet *big time* on the game. I'm the one placing a small TV in Matthew's lap. I'm in three and a half hours of prosthetic makeup to play Lazlo Gogolak in the sequel that Bruce offered me as I tanned on the beach in Hawaii. (No, that's not the back of Bruce's head as he touches up Matthew seconds before the camera rolls again; it's the makeup artist.)

"No, man, you're gonna come back as Janni Gogolak's father, Lazlo Gogolak. We're gonna put you in prosthetic makeup, you're gonna be even more insane, and it's gonna be fucking awesome."

"Holy shit, that sounds incredible! Is everybody coming back?"

"Everybody but Michael Clarke Duncan. That son of a bitch can suck my dick."

37

No Good Deed Goes Unpunished

Sometimes a friend gets involved in a smallish film project and will ask you to participate, with the implication that when it leads to something biggish, you'll get a call.

The first part, the part that helps my friends, happens all the time. The second part, the part that helps me, never fucking happens.

Ever.

The most frustrating part is that these so-called friends will hire actors who look enough like you to make you wonder why the fuck they didn't hire you in the first place. There are lots of people who have forsaken me thusly, but I shouldn't name names because they might just come around and I can't really . . .

Adam Shankman started his career as a choreographer, and I first meet him when Sarah Jessica Parker asks him to put together a little dance number on *Miami Rhapsody*. Adam is hilarious, and we get along swimmingly, so I'm pleased to reconnect with him a couple of years later when we both work on *She's All That,* a wonderful little movie that made a star of Freddie Prinze Jr. (Love Freddie, by the way. Tremendously sweet and humble, very down-to-earth fella.) Adam choreographs the big high school dance sequences with great style and to great success, I must admit. In 2001, Adam gets the chance to direct his own movie called *The Wedding Planner.*

He calls me up, tells me about the movie. "I've got three scenes for you. It's a small, thankless part, but I'd love for you to do it. Please do me this favor. It's my directorial debut, and if you do this, I'll never forget it. Please, please, please, say yes." And there it is, that implied *do-me-a-solid-and-I'll-hook-you-up later*. Naturally, because I like Adam and know that he's quite talented, I say yes.

I do the three scenes, two of which ultimately get cut. (To his credit, Adam calls to explain why they got cut and how it had nothing to do with me.) I'm onscreen for ninety seconds, and it looks like I'm the highest-paid extra in film history. Granted, the scene is just Matthew McConaughey and me, but come on. Horrifying.

I haven't gone through Adam's filmography lately, but I know he's directed a whole bunch of massive hits, and somewhere in one of them you'd think there was a part for little ol' me.

Oh, I know what you're thinking: *Hey, Kev, did you ever think that maybe your performance in Adam's film was shitty and that's why he hasn't called?* Fine, let's go with your version of the scenario, even though it's utterly ludicrous, if not proof that you're pathetic at the accusatory "Did You Ever Think . . ." hypothesis game.

So I stunk up the joint on the set of his first movie, but two factors take over from there:

(A) The movie's success rests on the shoulders of McConaughey and allowed pop star Jennifer Lopez to prove that she could also be a movie star. So, you see, he didn't need my less-than-movie-star status to sell any tickets.

(B) Let's face it, *I* don't give bad performances. I only end up in bad movies, which happens to the best of 'em. No way around it, we're all gonna end up in some real stinkers (more on that in a moment), but I beg you to point to one performance of mine wherein I truly stunk up the aforementioned joint.

No, I'm not being cocky. Name my performance wherein I'm horrible and write to me at Contact@KevinPollaksChatShow.com and we'll discuss it further.

So opening weekend, *The Wedding Planner* is number one at the box office; that same week, J-Lo's new album debuts at number one. Suddenly Jennifer Lopez isn't a singing and dancing pop star but rather a megasuperstar. What with all the money the film raked in, the über-talented Adam Shankman is, overnight, one of the most in-demand in the industry. Literally. And good for him. A terrific talent, no bullshit.

He's asked to direct again and again and again, but still no call to me. Nothing. Not even a hello, now that I think of it. But I wish the absolute best for Adam Shankman. That is, if by "best," I mean that, should he either read this or only be told about it and then recall how many times he used the word "*please*" way back when and finally make good on his promises to share the bounty of his success with the little people who helped make a complete unknown, unproven first-time director look good because he was able to call upon "friends" who had worked long and hard in the trenches to make enough of a name for themselves that first-time directors realized the upside of begging them to be in their first film—then, yes, I wish him the very best.

Bitter? Don't be silly.

38

Walken of Fame

It's always bizarre to encounter the people I impersonate. Meeting them was never the plan. The plan was just to mimic and/or mock them and then *never* meet them. Sometimes it works out wonderfully—Peter Falk at the grocery store—and sometimes, it's as surreal as life will ever get for me.

Like with Christopher Walken.

My agent tells me that Walken is being honored in Hollywood and I've been asked to participate. As you may or may not know, since the 1920s, the *really* big movie stars get their actual hands, feet, and signatures imprinted in cement in front of the Chinese Theater on Hollywood Boulevard. It's a huge honor that, these days, is bestowed only on a select few—mainly because they're running out of real estate.

They want me to be one of two speakers at the event; the other is Quentin Tarantino. Quentin directed him in *Pulp Fiction*, so they had a relationship. Me, I'd never met the guy. I was thrilled, of course, but I can't help but wonder how far down the list they had to go. I feel bad for Walken that I was the best they could come up with for his big day.

The day of, I'm led inside the theater, and, for the first time, I see Christopher Walken in the flesh . . . and I freak out. He turns, sees me, and his eyes pop with what appears to be either recognition or straight-up crazy.

"Heyyyyy!" he yells. "They told me. You. Were coming. Thannnks!"

It almost doesn't matter what he's saying because the whole time I'm thinking, *He's doing The Voice! And it's WAY better than mine.*

"Congratulations, Mr. Walken," I say, offering my hand. "This is a great honor."

He thanks me, then doesn't say another word. For ten minutes. Which, as it turns out, is a really fucking long time when no one's talking.

I'm nervous. He's odd. We're not talking.

At the end of these excruciating ten minutes, he turns to me and says, "Cement. Wo-ow!"

That's all. But really, who needs more?

Then the ceremony. Quentin speaks first, and Quentin speaks forever. (He'll talk until you shoot him in the head, that one.) Then, *finally*, it's my turn.

"The fact I'm here is odd," I say, "in that I was invited because I can impersonate the great man being honored. But I'd like to share this story with you.

"On Halloween, I love to scare the kids who ring my doorbell, so for the last few years I've been answering the door as Christopher Walken. I'll open it up, then gesture and pose like Christopher and say, 'Heyyyy! Trick or treat. Trick. Or treat. That's a damn good question. Quite the. Conundrum. You've put forth. On this. Hallow's Eve. Having said that, my young. Costumed friends. As fate would have it, I, *too,* have a question. Which one of you kids can guess. What I have. Buried. Under my house?'"

The press laughed, and that was nice, but seeing Chris bend forward at the waist and crack up was one of those *You can take me now* moments of perfection. Sweet, awkward, dreamlike, odd perfection.

39

Boldly I Go

"William Shatner is writing a new book about Trekkies called *Get a Life*, and he wants you to come to his office to work on one particular chapter, wherein *you* will describe for the reader how to do, in *his* opinion, the consummate Captain Kirk impression. He'd like you to help write this piece as a technical yet funny, step-by-step how-to manual."

That's how it's suggested to me that the time has finally come for me and the legend that is Bill Shatner to meet. Strange? Oh, sure. What would you do if you got that phone call from your agent, knowing that you had mocked Shatner for fifteen years on television, from Carson to HBO stand-up specials, not to mention twenty-five years of live stand-up shows all over North America?

Maybe, you might consider, *he's had enough, and he wants to kill you* . . .

You have to understand, for an idiot who does voices, this is as good as it gets. I dive into my car and race over to his office, repeatedly saying out loud: I can't believe this is happening!

Halfway there it dawns on me: Oh, nooooooooo. I'll have to say to his face, "Well, Mr. Shatner, sir, you were . . . a shitty actor. Yeah. You gestured like a marionette and took pauses no one could explain. I . . . I couldn't be the first to tell you this, sir, could I? Anyway, that's why there's an impersonation."

At a very young age, as I watched reruns of *Star Trek* with tremendous interest and loyalty, I couldn't help but notice that the actor portraying Captain James T. Kirk seemed . . . insane. The choices he made as an actor were riveting but bizarre, if not wildly theatrical and for no apparent reason. Or so it appeared to the eight-year-old me, anyway.

The style with which he strutted out of the elevator and onto the *bridge* of the *Enterprise*—chest first, square jaw locked in leadership, then coming to a stop. His right arm at a forty-five degree angle in front of his body swept left to right and back again like a pendulum. He stared at the alien *entity* on the screen before him, and then, after it *threatened* the well-being of his crew of over four hundred *brave* men and women, he thrust his hands forward, elbows six inches apart, and shouted "What gives you the *right?!*" with such absolute indignation that I *believed* the giant creature on the screen would reply:

"Whoa, shit, sorry. I didn't realize I was being such a dick"— ya know, but in their vernacular—"Let me rethink this whole seize-your-ship, kill-your-men, and enslave-your-women plan we had worked up. Clearly, I've misjudged you and your power. Yeah, so let me get back to my people and, um . . . Oh, *really* sorry about blasting your ship a bit ago, causing everyone to throw themselves from side-to-side in unison, the way they did. Which did not look fake at all, by the way."

I loved the show, and William Shatner was the juiciest serving of ham I had ever seen. Again, for the record, he was riveting to watch. Couldn't take your eyes off the crazy son of a bitch. But holy *crap*, were his teeth marks all over that scenery.

But Enough about You . . . William Shatner

I met Kevin Pollak head-to-head when he claimed he did me better than I do me. By God, he is right. So the person that you think is William Shatner is really Kevin Pollak. I on the other hand have taken on the lonely and unknown world of Kevin Pollak, and I am still looking for a job.

So I'm driving to his office, and I realize I can't shake his hand and suggest his acting style is ridiculous and that's why I've mocked him for a quarter century. But I've got to come up with *some* way to explain my technique of impersonating him. I want to be in the book. The following is what I make up in the car and present to William Shatner the first time we meet in his office:

"Well, sir, *Star Trek* was a great show, a phenomenal show, an amazing show . . . I certainly don't have to tell you that. (throat clear) It's just that, not *every* episode was great. And the set of the *Enterprise*, the bridge, was kind of cheesy looking. And the aliens that chased you around were pretty . . . lame. I remember that one albino-unicorn-*bear* looking thing . . . I mean what was *that?* (clear throat again) My point, sir, is that to us fans you weren't just the captain of the ship, you were captain of the show. I think in some episodes you had to create drama where there wasn't any, and I think in order to do that you may've had to . . . um . . . (my voice raises with fear) *overact* a little bit, ya know?"

It seemed like sound logic to me, and I believe to this day that's why he was gesturing like a lunatic and yelling at the poorly costumed creatures with conviction. I believe he believed that those moments would have just laid there if not for his melodramatic antics.

He agreed, too, because he printed my explanation verbatim. He also validated it as a theory by editorializing along with my text. You can get yourself a copy of his book if you want to read his comments, but I promise you his words that followed mine were such that he felt strongly that I had finally described *why* he did what he did on that show and went on to explain how his style, that I rationalized, was born years before during a run of a Broadway show.

The discovery I shared with him that day in his office must've stayed with him because it's now a part of his new one-man show, *Shatner's World: We Just Live in It,* a matinee of which is the occasion of our most recent run-in.

I'm in New York working at Carolines on Broadway, one of my favorite stand-up venues in the country. Rich Sommer, a terrific actor—he of *Mad Men* fame—came to see one of my shows. Afterward, I tell him that I had just found out that Shatner is doing a limited run on Broadway, and we agree to go to a matinee that Sunday. I e-mail Bill's office, arrange for tickets, and make reservations at my favorite brunch spot in New York, Bobby Flay's Mesa Grill—if you like southwest in your breakfast foods, it's to die for.

Rich and I are enjoying our preshow feast, when my cell phone vibrates from an incoming call. I look at the caller ID, and Rich asks if I need to get it, but I don't recognize the number, so no big woop. A little bit later, he excuses himself for a minute, so I listen to the voice mail.

"Ah, Kevin, it's Bill. I'm so happy you're coming to the show. Listen, just come to my dressing room about a half hour before curtain, and we'll discuss what we're going to do onstage together."

This is news.

As soon as Rich comes back, I play it for him, and I call Bill back.

"Hey, I got your message—sorry, I'm at brunch and didn't want to answer and be rude—and I can't wait to see the show tonight. Also, although I could truly not be more excited about this thing we're doing 'onstage together,' I'm sorry to report that your mentioning it in your call just now is the first I'm hearing of it."

Shatner explains, and soon enough Rich and I are in his dressing room discussing all that is and is about to be fantastic. Rich is having an out-of-body experience bearing witness to the proceedings, as he's already made it crystal clear to me what sort of fan he's been of Bill since childhood.

"OK, Kevin, so, you'll go to your seats," Shatner explains, "you'll watch the show, and then at about three minutes before the end, someone will tap you on the shoulder and then bring you backstage. I'll finish the show, hopefully to wild applause, during which I'll take a few bows and then hold up my hands, indicating I have an announcement. I'll tell them I have a special guest, you'll come out, and we'll, ya know, kibitz for a few minutes, get a few laughs, and then off we go. Sound fun?"

It's another *I can't believe this is happening* moment, clearly.

Rich and I take our seats, and the show begins. It's better than expected, but with the right amount of camp and oh-boy moments.

I'm, of course, as biased as a human can be about the show, and on this particular night I've lost all objectivity. I'll simply say that if you're a fan and you ever have a chance to see the show, run to get tickets and thank me later.

Three minutes until the finale, as explained, there's a tap on my shoulder, and a minute later I'm standing in the wings as Shatner finishes up. The crowd goes insane, a standing ovation, and then he calms them down with the news of a special guest.

"An old friend and a great actor/comedian is here. Please welcome Kevin Pollak."

I walk out using his walk, the *walk* that Captain James T. Kirk used as he made his way onto the bridge, and the crowd goes nuts. I'm hamming it up even more than he ever did, and they can't get enough. Once I reach him, I break the bit and tell him, in my own voice, how amazing the show was and how truly inspiring his performance is. The crowd cheers, but he's having none of it.

"No, no, please, Kevin, I thought we were just going to do a little shtick?"

Realizing that he's embarrassed by my genuine affection or prefers that I stop with the reviews and get to the funny, I turn toward the audience and say in my best Captain Kirk, "I've made a career out of . . ."

Hands thrust out, elbows six inches apart, frozen-in-time . . . 5, 6, 7, 8

". . . pausing!"

The crowd goes nuts again, Bill thanks me and the audience, and we stroll off into the wings, the captain and the mocking monkey.

Postscript

It was my first time on a Broadway stage, and I never imagined it would be so easy . . .

40

Jerry and Me

To say that Jerry Lewis is an influence is an obscene understatement. He's more than an influence—he's another one of those Mount Rushmore guys.

Jerry played the nincompoop in films—often as the ever-hip Dean Martin's sidekick—but in real life he was as cool as Dean. He became a gigantic movie star as a solo after the duo had risen to the apex of showbiz success, a success that can be equated only to the Beatles. I'm not joking. Go online if you're not old enough to remember—which actually I'm not, so I had to look it up my own damn self—because the Beatles are the only apt analogy.

There are photos and film footage all over the interwebs that validate this claim, so I'm just going to proceed. Think I'm lyin'? Spend eight minutes on Google, and stop yelling at me!

Jerry's duality—silly stage comedian and cool movie star/film director—is best exemplified by *The Nutty Professor*, a film about a nerdy teacher who drinks a magic potion and becomes a dashing heartbreaker. It touched a chord among filmgoers in part because every young man struggles to find his place in the world. Whether you want to be a famous funny person or you crave James Bond cool, you just want to fit in. (Hell, that horrible and at times life-threatening nonsense called Facebook is all about the basic human desire to be accepted as part of a community.) When I was a wee lad, my life was all about wanting to get laughs from being silly and dreaming of being popular with girls. Through his films and his life, Jerry Lewis showed it could be done.

In the fall of 2010, I get a call from my stand-up agent, Rich Super. (That's his real name, yes.)

"Jerry Lewis wants your telephone number. He wants to call you. Is that cool?"

"Give him the number." I couldn't spit the words out fast enough.

"Of course," he says. "I just wanted to make sure it was OK."

"Thank you. Now *give him the number!*"

Jerry calls a few days later while I'm in the shower; he leaves a voice mail: "Hi, Kevin. Jerry Lewis. Gimme a call. My number is (###) ###-####. I'll talk to you soon." An innocuous message, but I played it for all my friends because it's like a man on horseback has just hand-delivered a letter from Shakespeare.

I finally work up the nerve to call him back, I dial the number, and I have no idea where this number will take me. As it turns out, I end up in the last place I'd ever imagine: Jerry Lewis's living room.

"Helllllllooo?" he answers (himself).

"Um, hi, Jerry. It's, um, Kevin Pollak."

"*Kevin Pollak!*" Then, speaking as a nine-year-old: "*Oh, Kevin, yay yay, you called back!*" Then as a kind, sincere, mature man: "So, Kevin, I saw your stand-up special, and I have to tell you, it's the greatest thing I've seen in twenty-five years. Seriously, the best I've seen in a *very* long time. Truly. Better than Robin Williams, better than any of 'em, quite honestly. Blew me away. Listen, I've got some notes . . ."

When I hear Jerry search for his notes, I laugh out loud because he's just made the hippest misdirect joke I've heard in years. He set me up with the accolades and then tells me he's got "notes," which is performer lingo for, *I have a few ideas about how you might improve your act.* In this case, an act that's already been shot and edited and televised and can't be changed or improved. Oh, sorry, I just explained his joke. Oh, so now *I'm* the asshole . . .

My previous favorite misdirection joke comes from Garry Shandling: "So I'm dating this girl, she's gorgeous. Really. She's Ms. Georgia actually. Well, she's a *former* Ms. Georgia. Alright, it's George Foreman."

While I find the whole thing hilarious, it turns out Jerry's not joking. He's completely sincere.

"I wrote notes to myself," he says, "so that when we spoke I'd have a list of stuff right in front of me."

Then he goes through the list, point by point, and it's mesmerizing, surreal, and impossible to wrap my head around. He's so damn incisive that I'm having a difficult time staying focused on the fact that I'm speaking to The Jerry Lewis.

He goes through my act, citing specific moments, beats, nuances, and voices, comparing bits to moments from his and Dean's act. It's a dissertation that I was not prepared for. Even while critiquing me, he managed to be hilarious. "When you come out and spin the microphone stand to the left, do you have to join a separate union for that? *Very* smooth, though, Kevin. Marvelous."

After a couple of minutes, I have to remind myself to be present, to stop thinking about what kind of clever thing I'll say when Jerry gets done talking. That's where my brain automatically goes, by the way, always seeking the clever thing to say, especially when I first meet someone. If I'm ever introduced to you, dear reader, I might forget your name, and it's not because I don't care, but rather because as you're saying your name, I can't hear the words come out of your mouth thanks to the deafening little man in my brain who's seeking something clever to say the moment you finish talking. So, while Jerry's doing his thing, I'm forcing myself just to listen and focus entirely on him.

For once in your fucking life, I think, *just be present. A hero has reached out. Stop thinking, inhale, and embrace what this man from high atop Mount Olympus has chosen to impart, you lucky, fortunate idiot.*

"Thank you so much, Mr. Lewis," I say whenever he pauses to take a breath. "This means so much to me."

To which he always responds, "You're welcome. Call me Jerry."

He finishes the conversation by saying, "My father once told me that, if you see somebody you think is great, don't be afraid to reach out to him because otherwise he'll never know. So every now and then, I pick up the phone or write a letter, and I just wanted you to know that your stand-up special was the best thing I'd seen in twenty-five years, like I said. If you're ever in Vegas and you wanna stop by the office, we'll go have a bite to eat, we'll spritz some ideas for whatever, I don't know. Just know that I'm a big, big fan, and I always will be."

"That would be amazing, thanks. The second I can get to Vegas, I'll call you immediately. Would that be all right? Where should I call you?"

"Here. This number. This is my home. You have my number. So call it."

After we hang up, I do a little dance, and shout, "*Jerry fucking Lewis called! Jerry fucking Lewis called! Jerry fucking Lewis called!*"

Please understand: Acceptance and approval from that level of legend just don't happen to anyone, let alone to someone who had to sleep his way to the middle.

Three days later, another voice mail: "Hi, Kevin, Jerry Lewis. You'll never guess what was on TV today: *A Few Good Men.* I sat there and watched, and you were amazing. Call me back." I call him back, and he says, "Yeah, I just wanted to tell you that you were terrific in that film, and you know what was on between when I saw you in that and we're talking now? *Ricochet!*" It's only our second conversation, and the legend himself, The Mr. Jerry fucking Lewis, has become my mother. "So when're you coming to Vegas, darling?"

He calls everybody "darling." Don't get excited.

"As soon as I can, and I cannot *wait* to see you, Jerry."

Two days later, he calls again, and, for the three, seven, or nine of you marking your box scores, that's the third call in a week. "Kevin, Jerry Lewis. Listen, where do I get the special?"

"The what, now?"

"I've bragged to everybody I know here in Vegas that your special is the greatest thing I've ever seen, and now they all want to see it, so

I wanna have a little screening at the house. Where can I go to get a copy? I mean, it can't be out yet."

"Jerry, I have DVDs here. Why don't I send—"

"Oh, no, I didn't think it was out yet. I'll have my assistant find me a DVD of it at the store, then."

"Jerry, I'm happy to send you one. Please let me do that, really."

"Oh. OK. Ya have a pencil?"

As I take down the address, I ask, "Do I need a P.O. Box number?"

"No, that's my home. No one can believe I live here. You know, the last time I was on *Larry King*, he said, 'Jerry, why do you live in Las Vegas,' and I said, 'Because that's where my house is.'"

Now Jerry's doing bits for me. Fantastic.

Three days later, another call: "Kevin, everyone loves the special. Thank you so much for sending it. Listen, I wrote you a letter. I was gonna put it in the mail, but I was wondering if there's a fax number I can send it to you now instead."

A couple of weeks later, I'm booked to perform at a corporate function in Las Vegas. When I find out about the gig, I call Jerry and tell him I'm coming to town. We set up a lunch date at Olive's in the Bellagio. The day of, I arrive shortly before him and am ushered to the table reserved in his name. A bit later, he makes his entrance.

Jerry—who's closer to eighty-five than eighty—is accompanied by an assistant who's in his late-thirties. All of us shake hands, after which Jerry pulls me in for a hug. After a bit of small talk, some jokes, and a meal order, he goes back to being effusive and complimentary, then says, "Look, we brought you some gifts!"

The assistant hands over a bag imprinted with Jerry's logo. Inside are three Jerry Lewis DVD collections, and included is a note that says, "Kevin, I hope you'll have time to see some of the stuff that made me rich. Affectionately, Jerry Lewis."

At the bottom of a bag, there's a script. "What's this?"

"It's a movie I'm doing," he says. "I'm directing and starring, and I want you to play my son."

"When do we start?" I ask without hesitation.

"I think in the spring, but read the script, darling, then we'll talk."

It turns out the script is pretty terrific, a sweet comedy about a man whose wife died, and he has trouble moving on. Whenever Jerry's ready to start, I'm ready to start. I don't put all my eggs in the I'm-gonna-do-a-film-with-Jerry-Lewis basket, but it's always in the back of my head.

I don't hear from Jerry for a few months, but one morning I awake to an e-mail from his assistant: "Jerry wants you to know that the phone works both ways. You should give him a call."

An awkward note, but I ring Jerry, and he's as nice as ever. He apologizes for the delays with his film, explaining that he's backed up with other projects. "Listen, I'm gonna be out on my boat in San Diego for a couple of days . . ."

I'm having family in town and can't make it. He sounds hurt, but not terribly. "Sincerely, though," I say, "I'm unbelievably excited to see you again."

Over the next couple months, we speak a few more times, but, as is too often the case in showbiz, a new pal gets busy with life and work, and we fall out of touch. As of this writing, we haven't spoken for almost a year . . . but I still get a village idiot–size smile thinking about it.

Jerry fucking Lewis called! Jerry fucking Lewis called!

Postscript

Right before this book went to press, I landed a gig in Vegas, and Jerry and I are having another lunch at Olive's. This time, I'll try to get the check.

41

My Introduction to the Interwebs

When Jason Calacanis plays poker, he thinks it's hilarious to bring up topics and engage in shenanigans that he knows will annoy the fuck out of his opponents. Once on a huge stakes poker television show, he got so far under the skin of Daniel Negreanu—arguably one of the top five hold 'em players on the planet—that he manipulated him into calling a hand Negreanu *knew* was gonna cost him . . . and it did. Over 100,000 scoots. Anyone watching could tell that Negreanu was horrified that he had been bluffed by an asshole like Calacanis.

The first time I play with him, this Internet mini-mogul fuck from Brooklyn dives into some really, really horrible Christopher Walken impressions that he pretends—at least I think he's pretending—to think are brilliant and hilarious. He also drops shitty comments like, "Why'd you stop doing movies in the nineties?" (I will mention that since 2000, as of this writing, I've appeared in thirty-four films, so fuck him. Ya see, though, his nonsense still bothers me.)

Jason's tactic works way beyond his hopes; he gets under my skin, throws me off my game, and I lose big. He's so obnoxious that I later tell the host, "If that cocksucker is at the next game, don't bother inviting me."

But Enough about You . . . Sky Dayton

Kevin is a good friend whom I play poker with regularly. He should have named this book *How I Folded My Way to the Middle*. I've founded companies worth billions of dollars, but there isn't a day that goes by that I don't wish I was Kevin Pollak.

A few weeks later, Jason and I run into each other at another poker game, and, when I tell him just how much he annoyed the fuck out of me, he howls like a child then apologizes profusely, insisting that he's a huge fan and that he was acting like a dick to throw me off my game. A couple of days down the road, he e-mails asking if he can take me to lunch. I e-mail back, asking how the fuck he got my address, then tell him to take a very long walk off an extremely short pier. Later that week, I agree to meet him at the Santa Monica offices of his company, Mahalo.com.

At the time, Mahalo was an odd hybrid of Wikipedia and Google, a "people-driven web search." (With Google's algorithm system, nine out of ten times you search for a product, the first five hits have a deal with Google . . . but you didn't hear that from me.) Their offices look like the movie *Boiler Room*—no cubicles, just all these kids sitting at a long table, staring into computer screens, writing code. Jason sits in front of one of the many terminals, headset on his ears, speaking into a tiny mic attached to the headset, looking like a bloated, white, two-left-feet-havin' *Rhythm Nation*–era Janet Jackson.

I peek over his shoulder. He's holding a Q&A with his online minions. Jason's a self-made success story in the Internet world, and if you're a 'net nerd, you know who he is. In fact, he may be one of your heroes, and that abso-fucking-lutely *kills* me. Meanwhile, the way things are headed, the geek shall inherit the earth.

The questions are ridiculous; the answers, more so.

jason, wut kind of cereal do u like?

I prefer Rice Krispies. As a matter of fact, I prefer Kellogg's products in general because the history of the company is simply fascinating. Founded in Battle Creek, Michigan, in 1906 by Will Keith Kellogg, it was an outgrowth of his brother John's work at the Battle Creek Sanitarium. I could go on for days about this, but I have limited time.

And so on.

As Calacanis entertains the nerds, I make my presence known. He grabs me a chair and motions for me to sit down. Then he says into his mic: "Award-winning actor Kevin Pollak is here." He pulls me into the camera's view, and I give a little wave, realizing that this is the first time that I've used any kind of video-chat setup.

Don't get me wrong: I wasn't a complete technophobe. Actually, I'd been part of the computer age for years, ever since I played Pong and Space Invaders in between my stand-up sets at all those shitkicker bars. I'd also been suckling on the Apple teat ever since I bought my first tower in 1984. I've had at least twenty Mac computers since, and the only iteration I didn't purchase was that ridiculous colored bubble iMac piece of shit.

Today, I make sure I have all Apple products on the day they hit the stores, and, as I write this, I'm futzing with my iPhone 4S with the updated 4G network.

| Here's fun for ya: Tell Siri, "I need to get rid of a body."

The irony, though, is that, despite being such an Apple devotee, I'm not, nor have I ever been, a tech guy. I just like having cool fucking toys that I use only for writing, info/news searching, light shopping, and, of course, e-mailing.

Jason leans over and covers his mic. "I signed you up on Twitter, by the way."

"Thanks. I can't wait to find out what that means." I'd heard of Twitter, but in that moment, in February 2009, I don't know anybody who partakes. Still, I'm intrigued.

As Calacanis goes back to his chat, the notion of a real-time online community in which I can interact directly with my fan base begins to intrigue me. As a comedian, it's always been about the immediate, real-time reaction from the audience, and one of the drags about movies is that I miss that instant feedback, that simultaneous connection. Years ago, I had to come to terms that it'll always kinda suck to be funny in a movie, then have to wait ten months for the laugh in theaters.

I also realize that if I use the computer to connect to my audience, I don't have to leave my house. I'm pretty damn lazy, so this is kind of perfect.

When Jason finishes chatting, he shows me around the facility. I can't help but tune out the techie part of his tour because the second my brain hears something it doesn't understand, it shrinks. But then we arrive in this 20x20 studio, replete with lights, cameras, and a green screen wall.

"What the hell is this?"

"Um, a studio that one of my guys uses to . . ."

But I don't absorb the rest of what he said because that brain of mine is screaming with ideas about what I can do with this space. I can shoot comedy bit, after comedy bit, after comedy bit. I can use the green screen to do fake ski reports. I can do . . . anything.

Then, once again of its own accord, my mouth moves. Before I can stop it, it says, "Hey, I think I wanna do a fun version of *Charlie Rose* from here."

Those words, in that order, had never entered my head. Sure, if you were a stand-up during the Johnny Carson era, you'd always dreamed that at some point in your career you *might* get to host a talk show—and if you don't admit to that, you're a liar—but you never honestly believe it'll happen.

Jason stops mid-sentence—or at least I think he was in mid-sentence; I wasn't really listening to what he was saying. He's a talker—

"How soon can you start?"

That fucking Calacanis . . .

But Enough about You . . . Jason Calacanis

I first met Kevin Pollak at one of the countless poker games taking place in Los Angeles on any given weeknight. I knew exactly who he was and had seen a dozen of his films. In fact, I was a bit of a fan.

Being the ball buster I am at the poker table, I figured I would try and tweak him. One of the great things about celebrities is that if you pretend not to know who they are they get completely tilted.

So I waited for the perfect moment. About an hour into the game I said: "You look familiar. What do you do?"

"I'm in the entertainment business," deadpanned Kevin.

"Oh yeah, you were in a bunch of movies in the eighties and nineties right?"

He smiled and nodded.

"What have you been doing since then?"

Zing! Pow!

He laughed, we all laughed, and I figured I would try and take it up a notch.

"You know, I did see you in an awesome film recently."

Again, a smile and nod from Kevin. He knew what was coming. I glanced down at Kevin's IMDB page looking for the worst film he had ever been in.

"You were awesome in . . . *Juwanna Man.*"

"Ha! Ha. Ha!!!" a classic Kevin Pollak laugh.

After a couple of games together, it got so bad that Kevin actually told one of the hosts to let him know when I was playing—so that he could sit that game out. But a friendship was born. A friendship based on the mutual enjoyment of two things: the intersection of technology and media as well as a passion for busting balls—specifically at poker tables.

Without knowing it, my ball-busting antics were actually a shadow of the breaking of the balls that Kevin had been known for. After Kevin's initial disdain for me, we turned our ball-busting into a tag-teaming of other poker players. It was brilliant. We crushed people, and hours and hours of laughter later I invited Kevin to come by the office of my technology start-up.

We set Kevin up on Twitter, then we played with some new live video streaming technology in my office. Instantly hundreds and then thousands of Internet users started interacting with Kevin on a live stream from my office. A large amount of Diet Coke spewed from the nostrils of geeks all across the interwebs that day.

Fuck! This guy is made for the Internet, I thought to myself.

A couple of weeks later we launched *Kevin Pollak's Chat Show,* one of the first streaming video shows ever created. Now, over the years I've seen many celebs get interested in technology, only to balk when they heard that it paid little compared to their day jobs. Most couldn't be bothered to understand the medium, let alone where it was going.

Kevin was the opposite. He didn't care about the money, but he did care about how we were innovating. Could we incorporate Twitter and his fans into the show some way? Could we take questions from the audience? When would HD streaming arrive? Could iPhone users tune in on their 3G connections or only if they had Wi-Fi?

His interviews with directors, actors, and comedians are classics that will become the interviews of record for some of the most talented entertainers of our time. Kevin's warmth and insights have transformed the standard "two anecdotes and a plug" interview format, into two- and three-hour raucous and insightful tombs for the ages. He's a true pioneer of this new medium, and a hundred years from now folks will be studying his interviews to try and figure out what life was like during the turn of the century.

Oh yeah, and he was awesome in *The Santa Clause 2.* Seriously, Netflix it.

Postscript

As I write this, <u>Kevin Pollak's Chat Show</u> is celebrating its three-year anniversary. Our guest was my ol' pal, Ed Begley Jr.

Wait. I just gave away the ending of the next chapter. Shit.

You know what? Blame that fucking Calacanis . . .

But Enough about You . . . Henry Winkler

Working with Kevin Pollak is like water-skiing on a smooth lake at five in the afternoon at a resort in the Northeast. In other words, it's a comfortable and articulate and exciting experience. I'm talking about how easy he made me feel sitting across the table from him when we chatted for a mere two hours during his *Chat Show.* He brings out the best in you because one of his greatest attributes, besides being very funny, is that he is a good listener. And no, we never kissed.

42

If You're Not Creating, You're Waiting

The day after I visit Mahalo and Calacanis (aka The Mad Greek) says *Go, man, go, Kevin Pollak's Chat Show* takes over my life. Preparation for the launch goes relatively smoothly, but it's a learning process for us all. For instance, I didn't think I'd want or need a sidekick on a show like this.

Enter Samm Levine.

I meet Samm when I cold-call his manager after my girlfriend Jaime and I start watching *Freaks and Geeks* on DVD. Why did you two begin watching *Freaks and Geeks* at this late date, you might ask? Because she wants to and I always meant to. Also, a number of people had told me, There's a guy on the show who's like a younger version of you. That guy was Samm; thus the cold call.

Turns out Samm is a huge fan and insists that we'd met previously at the Friars Roast of Rob Reiner—which I didn't believe until he provided photographic evidence. After several meals and poker nights together, we become fast friends, so when I tell Samm about *KPCS*, he says, "How would you feel about a sidekick?"

"I don't think it's really that kind of show. I'm thinking of having Jaime on camera—but not at the table—while she feeds me the live Twitter questions to test it out. If you're serious, maybe you could sit next to her and we could banter."

He agrees, and we're off. Wrangling one of the many key members of our behind-the-scenes crew was just as easy.

Since I don't know shit from Shinola about tech stuff, I have to find people who do, and my first hire is Jason McIntyre. J-Mac was a drama major from Pittsburgh who, like many aspiring actors, had his dreams of stardom shattered on the rocks of bourbon. (Kidding.) He's a fine fella who's quite talented and funny, a great friend of Jaime's from back in Pitt—same college and servers at the same restaurants—and has become a true friend, not to mention a damn good poker dealer.

During my techie search, I learn there's a small production community/subculture that specializes in original online content. I beg a few of them to join Team *Chat Show*, then snag a couple others from Mahalo.com, and we jump in face-first.

"Shouldn't I ask my publicist to gear up the machine?" I ask Calacanis before our first show.

"The only marketing we need for this launch are your Tweets," Jason insists.

As is the case whenever he tries to school me on how things work in this brave new interwebs world, I tell him, "My world of *real* show business is better because it's been around longer and therefore proven."

After dozens of similar conversations, though, I begin to see the light. The old world order has led to heaps of frustration, and it might be time to embrace this new paradigm.

So I listen to the jerk.

We stream our first live show on March 22, 2009, at 5:00 p.m., PDT, with LeVar Burton as our first guest. Not only is LeVar our first guest, but he's the first guest we book via Twitter, now a regular occurrence for us. Other Twitter invitees: Fred Savage, Chris Pratt, Nathan Fillion, and Michael McKean.

Then I find out only fifteen hundred people watched.

"Great numbers, Calacanis," I snarl. "Way to promote."

He smiles. "Just wait."

Six weeks after our marketed-on-Twitter-only launch, a *Los Angeles Times* reporter comes to interview me and my modest crew. A few days later, we're in column one on the front page. To give those of you outside L.A. a little perspective, column one on the *Times* front page is never showbiz related, unless, that is, one of us showbiz types rapes or murders someone . . . or, in the case of the column one story that ran the day after ours, one of our own—in this case Michael Jackson—dies. True.

I must know three hundred people in L.A. Guess how many of them told me they'd read the article. If you answered, "seven," you'd be correct. But it gets more pathetic from there. Four of those seven read it online. Point being, nobody reads the *L.A. Times.* Ain't that a bitch?

At first, when I talk to people about my online-only show, there's a pervasive sense of *If you can't make it in showbiz, you can make it on the Internet.* (A lot of people thriving in traditional media absolutely feel that way to this day.) But I keep plugging ahead, and about six months in I'm invited to speak on some panels . . . which is unfortunate for them because I don't know dick about squat. Still, my ego is such that if anyone asks me to speak about anything, I'm pretty much there. At these talks, I learn that when somebody with my traditional media street cred moves into the online realm, they're embraced with tears of gratitude.

But Enough about You . . . Damon Lindelof

Kevin Pollak is a master of the great art of conversation, a gifted storyteller who has a way of coaxing even the most uncomfortably personal confessions from those he sits across from. He is a modern day Dick Cavett, and what few realize is that Kevin killed Dick Cavett and ate his heart in order to attain his essence. I would sit down with him anytime, anywhere . . . not just because I will learn more about myself in the process, but because I am deeply and profoundly afraid of what he would do to me if I refused.

A year and a half into the run, after more of my complaining about numbers, Calacanis tells me: "We're not too far from having the Internet on television. Once you can access the Internet from the remote control, that's when it changes. This is a pioneering era, Kevin, and you're part of it. So stop whining."

Sure enough, companies like Samsung are now selling new flatscreens with the Internet built into the remote control, not to mention Apple TV, Roku . . . hell, TiVo allows people to watch the *Chat Show*. Fans of the show tell me time and again that they love watching us on their big ol' television. Again, Calacanis was on target, the son of a bitch. So much so, in fact, that this last bit will read prehistoric in less than a year.

In creating content for the Internet, I enjoy complete creative freedom, and, most importantly, complete control of everything I create—neither of which I've had since I was back in San Jose, making up stand-up stuff, bringing it to a dark stage, and delivering to twenty-seven people. Then there's the sense of ownership. Your web creation is, and always will be, yours. Even if you get sponsors to pony up, you still own the content. Having full ownership and control of your ideas, bits, sketches, stories, or, in my case, conversations, simply doesn't exist in traditional media.

In early 2012, Hulu.com licensed the entire *Chat Show* library as well as any future episodes, a tremendous shot in the arm to me and my mighty crew. Hulu reaches over twenty million people a day. Later that spring, we hit a milestone when the episode with Sugar Ray Leonard

But Enough about You . . . Mark Cuban

I've always admired Kevin as an actor and comedian. Never enough to listen to or watch his podcast, though. Or maybe just listen. Is his podcast even available on video? Anyhow, Kevin has definitely been able to turn something that no one wants—a podcast—into something that at least some people watch or listen to. In a world of unlimited choices, making something out of nothing is an amazing talent, and Kevin definitely is an amazing talent.

drew 85,000 live views—Internet-speak for people watching the show live throughout the two-plus hours. For live Internet content, that's an astounding number. Our entire archive is available on iTunes, where we average several hundred thousand downloads a month; a few times, we've even cracked the million downloads in a month mark.

I sincerely hope this doesn't come off as bragging. Yes, I'm a narcissist, but I share this with you, dear reader, only because I still can't believe this is happening. It just demonstrates that if you're not creating, you're waiting. When you create online content, you can do anything you want. Your only limit is your imagination.

Unless, of course, you're in the porn business.

EPILOGUE
President Clinton's Superpowers

From the day he first entered the national public consciousness, I've been a fan of Bill Clinton. I mention this for a very important reason, but in order to build up the dramatic tension I'm not going to tell you what.

Steve Martin and I get along well during *L.A. Story*, but we never become close; nonetheless, whenever I run into him over the ensuing years, he's always warm and friendly. We don't work together again until the summer of 2010, when we shoot a bird-watching comedy called *The Big Year*. It has a huge cast—Jack Black, Anjelica Huston, Rashida Jones, Joel McHale, Dianne Wiest, and Owen Wilson among *many* others—but all of my scenes are with Steve Martin and Joel McHale. Again, not too shabby.

Early on in the shoot, Joel confesses to me that he's a *huge* fan of Steve, and he's like a little kid about the whole thing. "Do you think he'll have lunch with us?" he asks breathlessly. "Do you think he'll want to hang out with us? Do you think we'll become friends? Do you think, do you think, do you think?" He was trying to make me laugh, which he did, but his interest was 100 percent genuine.

"I don't know, Joel."

Hanging out with the big, gigantic, enormous star of the movie is never anything I've sought out, as you know by now. It's out of respect more than anything; I don't want to presume that while shooting *Grumpier Old Men*, Sophia Loren wants to grab a bite.

But Joel can't hold back, so after our first morning of shooting he blurts out to Steve, "Kevin said you'd want to have lunch with us!"

"Did I?" I say.

Steve smiles. "That's a great idea." So each day, for the remainder of our time on the movie together, the three of us share a meal, whether we're shooting in Vancouver or New York. New York is especially good for Steve because he lives there (as well as Los Angeles), and he knows all the best restaurants. Plus, having him in our party makes it pretty easy to get a table, not to mention there's less of a chance that Joel will stick me with the check.

> A highlight of our time together: Joel and I kinda forced Steve to sign up for Twitter. So if you enjoy following @SteveMartinToGo, you're welcome.

After we wrap, Steve and I stay sort of in touch via e-mail, but, as is often the case with movie friends, absence makes the mind grow absent, so after a while the e-mails get spaced further apart, and it's on to the next project, on to the next new friend.

But that's only most of the time.

A couple of months later, I wake up to an e-mail from Steve, letting me know that his friend, singer James Taylor, is hosting the 120th Anniversary Gala of Carnegie Hall and Steve's recommended me as someone who can do a tribute to Lenny Bruce's midnight concert there in 1963.

That's one helluva wonderful gesture, but here's the thing: I'd never done Lenny Bruce. It wasn't like I was this huge fan, even. I have tremendous respect and appreciation for him—if you're a comedian with a soul, you can't help it—but he wasn't one of my big influences because, by the time I started paying attention to stand-up around 1967, Lenny wasn't allowed to be on television, thanks in part to his many, many obscenity arrests. Besides, I was more into comics such as Bill Cosby, and that's about as far from Lenny as you can travel. I couldn't get with Lenny's spicy mustard because I was *ten years old.*

Six weeks later: *Ring* . . . er, rather: *vvvvviiiiibbbbbrrrrraaaaattttte.*

"Hello?"

"Hey, man, this is James Taylor."

"Hey, James, yes, hello . . ." Oh, geez. I wasn't instantly nervous as hell. I mean, what the hell, man?

"So Steve said you might be up for doing this thing for us at Carnegie?"

"Oh, *did* he, that presumptuous son of a bitch," I say, recovering quickly.

He laughs. Thankfully.

James explains that he's been asked by the Carnegie Hall committee, or foundation, or whatever the hell they call themselves, to stage a few shows celebrating the 120th anniversary. Bette Midler is on board for a Sophie Tucker tribute; Sting is doing a Beatles tribute; Steve is doing a Flatt and Scruggs tribute; and James hoped I could recreate a few minutes of Lenny Bruce, who had a rather amazing and fairly historic midnight show there, three weeks after the JFK assassination.

I agree instantly, not knowing whether I can actually pull this off. It's the old scene that actors all know about, where the director asks the actor, prior to hiring him or her, "Gosh, you know, you're really perfect for this part, but can you ride horseback?" The hungry actor responds, "Are you kidding, I've got a saddle in my trunk!"

James and I discuss how the selection of Lenny's routine might work, and we both agree that Steve should weigh in immediately. He thanks me a few more times, and I assure him that it's he who's doing the favor here and, if I'm a disappointment in any way, it should be Steve who gets the blame.

"Well," James says, "Steve wants to introduce you on the night, and then you'll come out and do a few minutes of Lenny's act. I don't know what part of his routine or bit you want to do, but you certainly have a couple of months to figure it out."

So I get to work.

First thing I do is e-mail Steve and thank him and ask him to call me so we can discuss; hopefully he'll offer suggestions as to which of Lenny's bits would work. While I wait for Steve's reply, I dive into the Lenny library.

I have to stick to a few parameters put forth by James, the most important of which is that the bit can't be more than five minutes long. You'd think that would be easy, but . . . no. All of Lenny's bits are either two minutes, nine minutes, or fifteen hours. Also, Lenny didn't do punch lines, so nothing ended on a laugh; the recorded bits ended when the recording engineer faded out the track. This is a problem because, as every comic knows, Rule #6 in the Official American Comedian's Handbook is: Leave 'em on a laugh. There's no way I'm going to play Carnegie Hall for the first time in my career without leaving on a laugh.

> I'm sorry, did I not mention that this would be my first time performing onstage at arguably the most revered venue in the country? Yeah.

I assume Steve is familiar with Rule #6, so when he calls, I let my concerns be known.

"Do you have a favorite Lenny bit in mind?" he asks.

I say that I'm having some difficulty.

Steve then proceeds to give me one of the most brilliant pieces of advice: "You should probably do one of the funny ones."

"Yeah, I guess that makes sense," I laugh.

"I'm serious, actually. What I mean is, don't do any of the druggie material, or the political stuff, or 'How to Entertain Your Colored Friends at Parties.'"

> "How to Entertain . . ." is a classic piece of racist deconstruction that, if performed today, would probably be more controversial than when he debuted it in the early-1960s. Even if an extremely well-liked and respected white comic said what Lenny did in this bit, he'd be burned in effigy.

"It's just that this is a fund-raiser," Steve continues, "and the crowd's probably going to be a tad older, so something like, well, you know, Lenny had a lot of really funny non-offensive stuff." He does three or four of Lenny's routines verbatim, most of which I'd heard quite recently while doing research, and his accuracy is impeccable, as if he'd been listening to them just prior to our call, which, of course, he hadn't.

I end up choosing a piece in which Lenny discusses an appearance on *The Steve Allen Show*. In the bit, as was Lenny's wont, he kvetched about censors and how they wouldn't allow him to perform a particular story he wanted to tell on the show; this piece in question was about his tattoo. His monologue included a reference to his aunt, who he claimed sounded like "a Jewish seagull," and a thread about the concept that Jews with tattoos can't be buried in a Jewish ceremony because of the belief that you have to go out of the world the way you came into it—which of course doesn't stop circumcision.

It was funny, smart, and honest—the perfect summation of what Lenny was all about—*and* it was clean.

Once I make my decision, I'm ready. I'm hyped. I can't wait to get onto that hallowed stage. But there's that minor, little, teeny, tiny issue of sounding like Lenny.

Most of my impressions come to me naturally, but I can't get the Lenny movement, gestures, and physical nuances from the records, of course, so step one was to track down some footage of him at work. The problem there is, I can only find two pieces of video, both performances on *The Steve Allen Show*, funnily enough. From them, I pick up how he moved his hands, legs, hips, and head, and eventually I'm able to recreate his jazz-like, staccato delivery. It takes a while to get it right, but I get it . . . or at least I hope I do.

For the next few weeks, I Lenny around the house . . . but only when alone. I don't want anybody to hear it until show night. Jaime ends up catching me several times, but she's used to me walking around the house, speaking in tongues.

The day before the performance, there's a tech rehearsal at Carnegie to make sure the music and lighting cues are set, and Bette Midler's and Sting's respective numbers sound perfect. The producer asks me to run down my piece, and I quickly say that I'd rather not have the only memory of performing the piece prior to showtime be for the nine people seated in the audience. It's not the vision I want to take to the stage the following evening. He seems to understand.

But Enough about You . . . Adam Richman

Being safely ensconced on the G-list of Hollywood as a basic-cable food host, I feel, gives me safe distance to throw stones at a friend I deeply admire and respect who has worked with Levinson, Reiner, Nicholson, et al.

I met Kev for the first time for a dinner double-date in Brooklyn with his lovely better half. Much like me, he's a Jew fighting hair loss who punches out of his weight class and gets beautiful women to love him. Unlike me, his Walken impression is effortless and amazing, not to mention Johnny Carson and Peter Falk. I foolishly attempted *my* Walken at dinner. Kev looked at me like an art student who suggested to Michelangelo that he might want to use more red on the ceiling. My bad.

He was gracious enough to make a cameo on my show. He was equally gracious enough to hijack my trailer as his own and my assistant as his own, and charismatic and talented enough to make my crew wish that they worked for and with him rather than the G-lister whose crap you're reading now. He's every bit as talented as you think he is, *almost* as talented as he thinks he is, and an infuriatingly nice, gracious, warm, and generous human being. But he can't describe a taco for shit. I don't have solid impressions, sixty-plus movies under my belt, or a cool lovely missus like he does, so I cling to that.

Mmmm . . . tacos. (Don't judge me.)

Steve asks for a sit-down so we can come up with some stage banter for my introduction . . . plus, as I learned during that lunch, he wants to protect me. Over salads, he says, "I really want the audience to love you before you start the Lenny bit, so I'd like to set the scene by having you do a couple of impressions. We'll talk, you'll do some Christopher Walken, maybe a few others, and this way the people can get a flavor of *you*—the actor they know. They'll also see you do impressions that they'll instantly recognize, so even before you do Lenny, they'll accept you. Nobody will wonder why we had a character actor do this."

I agree and tell him that, since there's a good chance they won't really remember what Lenny sounds like, this is a tremendous help to me. It's wildly insightful of Steve to know this about any audience, and, as he shares this plan, two things race through my mind: *Wow, he's really looking out for me, which is amazingly cool.* Make no mistake, this is one of the most generous things that any fellow comedian has ever done for me—protect me, make sure that I'm in a good place, and that the crowd is on my side.

The second thought in my noggin is, *Holy shit, I'm gonna spritz with another Mount Rushmore guy!* We eventually come up with some nice patter:

STEVE MARTIN walks alone onto the bare stage.

                    STEVE
You've heard some great music tonight,
and you're going to hear a lot more. But
there were also a lot of great comedy
shows here at Carnegie Hall as well.

STEVE points to the wall behind him, on which giant pictures of Bob Hope, George Carlin, Jimmy Durante, and others are projected.

STEVE
Hey, I did a show here, actually, in
1978. I should be on that wall somewhere
. . .

*STEVE turns around and looks at the back
wall . . . and a tiny photo of him, about
1/100th the size of the others, appears in
the lower right corner.*

Oh, there it is. Anyway, when I was
growing up, a lot of my friends would
listen to music while they were falling
asleep at night. Me, I used to listen to
comedy albums, and one of my favorites
was Lenny Bruce. Lenny did a famous
midnight show here in 1963 that became a
best-selling record. There was a massive
snowstorm that night, and nobody was
expected to show, but it turned out the
place was packed. We wanted to have
somebody recreate a bit of what happened
that night, so I've asked my friend
comedian/actor Kevin Pollak, who does
wonderful impressions, to come out and
give us a couple minutes. Oh, Kevin!

*KEVIN POLLAK walks onto the stage. The crowd
applauds. He looks into the audience, where,
naturally, nobody is standing.*

KEVIN
Please be seated. That's too kind.

                    STEVE
So, Kevin, you like to do
impersonations.

                    KEVIN
          (As Christopher Walken)
Yes, Steve. Gotta tell ya. I'm excited
to. Be heah this. Evening. Wo-ow.

                    STEVE
Would you mind doing one now?

                    KEVIN
     (Does a take to the audience, and
          then, as himself)
Well, I like to do esoteric ones, off
the beaten track.

                    STEVE
Like who?

                    KEVIN
Like Alan Arkin.

                    STEVE
Oh, wow . . . really?

                    KEVIN
              (as Arkin)
Let me tell ya, Steve, it's a great
night, but I'm sittin' way up there, and
I can't see anythin'. You would think
I'd have a better seat.

STEVE
Kevin, let me ask you, do you ever do
really famous people?

STEVE gestures to himself, not-so subtly.

KEVIN
Oh, I never thought of this before, but
has anybody ever impersonated you?

STEVE
Well actually, no.

KEVIN
I wouldn't worry about that. Usually the
person has to have a, um—

STEVE
Unique voice?

KEVIN
. . . personality.

STEVE
Ladies and gentleman, a few minutes with
Lenny Bruce.

*STEVE leaves the stage, and KEVIN becomes
Lenny.*

After lunch, we rehearse our bit on the Carnegie stage, and I decide to
do a couple of sentences of the Lenny piece, but before I know it I've

Steve and I doing Hope and Crosby at Carnegie Hall. Steve gave me a chance to shine before my tribute to Lenny Bruce, and I took it, damn it.

done the entire routine. In front of nine people. I just can't stop. As it turns out, thank the heavens I didn't—because when I walk offstage Steve asks, "Can I make a few suggestions?"

"Of course."

"OK. When I walk offstage, you should turn and watch me, so you're no longer facing the audience. Then there should be a lighting change to alter the mood, and as that's happening you should do something physical, even if it's just slumping your shoulders an inch, some sort of transition before you turn to face the audience *as* Lenny Bruce. I think theatrically, that would help."

Would I have come up with that myself? Absolutely not. While I'm wrapped up in getting Lenny's voice, Steve's thinking about creating the end of Pollak and the beginning of Bruce. Sure, it's about giving his friend James Taylor the best show possible, but, again, it was about protecting me.

Getting notes from Mount Rushmore: priceless.

Next up, show night!

As I'm standing in the wings while Steve introduces me, I feel a pounding in my throat that I'd never experienced. I'm always excited, but tonight I'm *truly* nervous when Steve brings me out.

I needn't have worried. First off, our banter goes over like gang-busters. It feels like a new kind of special, doing Hope and Crosby shtick with the likes of Steve Martin. *Huge* laughs. As for my Lenny tribute, in my mind, the four-minute bit lasts four seconds, in the middle of which, it hits me: *Holy shit, I'm performing a routine for the first time onstage, and I'm doing it onstage at Carnegie fucking Hall. It's official: I've lost my mind.*

It's surreal and fantastic, better than I imagined, a true career high-light. After I finish, I get all kinds of thanks and congrats from James and others and make my way to the back of the hall so I can watch the rest of the show. That's right, folks, I didn't have a seat. My girlfriend and her family, yes. My cousin Terry Zucker—who got us all into this mess all those years ago with the Dave Clark Five in the Circle Square Theater in San Carlos, California—yes. My friends Sam Robards and his wife, Sidsel, yes. Me? Nope. I don't mind, though. I'm way too wound up after doing the impossible that I'm incapable of sitting still. Plus, watching the show from the back and being able to move to the backstage area at will are more to my liking.

Near the end of the night, a surprise guest struts onto the stage: (former) President Bill Clinton. In that drawl that I've always enjoyed channeling, he says, "I was a bit of a musician myself for many years, but of course I never got to play Carnegie Hall. I was never good enough. But I always dreamt of it, so I'd like to thank James Taylor for having me here. Just to stand on this stage is good enough. James has been a great friend of mine and my wife Hillary's, and he's never asked me to do anything ever. Until tonight, that is, and it's my honor."

He goes on to talk about how the money the show has raised was for underprivileged kids to study music, who will now have a chance to perform at Carnegie as he never got to. It was inspiring. Oh, he's *good*.

This is why Bill Clinton is one of the few politicians I've ever liked. When he speaks about "our children's future," I believe he genuinely gives a damn. As he was halfway through his remarks, another one of those ballsy ideas entered my skull. It was a revelation even, you might say.

I'd been coming and going to and from backstage for the past two days, and I knew the route, so I drew a mental map and deduced that if I positioned myself six feet one inch from the back of the curtain and three feet seven inches from the front of the elevator, then Clinton would be forced to walk past me and possibly to "run into me." Maybe I'd get a nod, which would've been more than enough.

Once in my spot, I wait for the former president to finish. Four Secret Service guys eye me up and down, but they know I've been on stage earlier and deduce—accurately, as it turns out—that taking out Clinton tonight wouldn't be the best career move.

Clinton wraps up his address to loud and vigorous applause, then, after a few photos with those in the wings, heads my way. Well, not my way exactly, but toward the elevator, by which I had positioned myself so that he'd probably at least see me.

I adjust my body so that I'm not in the Secret Service sight line, but not to the point that I'm completely out of the president's path. Clinton follows his Servicemen, then glances in my direction. I tense up a smidge and wait for the nod.

It doesn't happen.

Instead, he makes a beeline right to me, comes to a dead halt, and takes my hand in both of his. "Kevin, I'm a big, big fan of yours and have been for a long time, and I was a fan of Lenny's growing up."— meaningful pause—"He was here tonight. Thank you."

Another meaningful pause and then he smiles. "By the way, that thing you feel in your mouth? That's my penis."

Wait, what?!

Look, I'm not saying that last part happened. I don't know what the hell happened, to be honest. I don't remember my feet touching the ground as he spoke. People, there's a missing ninety-seven seconds in my memory . . . I cannot confirm or deny exactly what took place beyond "He was here tonight. Thank you."

I smile and nod as he speaks, not wanting to say anything stupid. Eventually I utter something, but it's worthless filler with no point or consequence. He never lets on that I'm not really contributing to the conversation but rather accepts his responsibilities as the reason that it was a moment.

That ability that Clinton has to make whomever he's talking to feel all important, I don't know if it's a gift—or maybe an old grifter's skill—but it doesn't matter really. I *am* the only person he's talking to in those couple minutes, and without question I feel more special than anyone else on the planet.

Later that night I think, *Once again, you maniac, a historic life moment came to pass because you took the reins and created it.* I could've stayed at the back of the hall and watched him finish his speech and been as moved as everyone else in the room, and that would've been a great story in and of itself.

But I like how the story happened better mostly because I forced myself in it.

ACKNOWLEDGMENTS

Along with my sincerest thanks to all of whom I've written about and who participated in the *But Enough about You* sections, as well as the two forewords and quotes for the book jacket, I want to offer a very special thanks to the following people, without whom I'd still be doing Bill Cosby's album for $10.

My mom, Elayne, and her husband, Dick Harlow; my dad, Robert Pollak; my brother, Craig; Kitty, Jason, and Courtney Pollak; Randy, Terry, Ron, Shirley, and Sylvan Zucker; Craig Singer, Chuck Leiter, Jon Scott and Larry Tract, Lucy Webb, Peter Nelson, Jim Walters, Steve Marks, Leigh Brillstein, George Freeman, Nikki Joel, Arthur Spivak, Rich Super, George Ruiz, Matt Luber, Merv Griffin, Johnny Carson, Jim McCauley, David Letterman, Larry King, Albert Brooks, Steve Martin, James Taylor, Bruce Willis, David Steinberg, Don Rickles, Rich Little, Les Moonves, Nina Tassler, Bernie Brillstein, Jason Calacanis, James Jayo, Jason Allen Ashlock, Alan Goldsher, Elaine Ewing, Corey Levin, Jason McIntyre, Josh Negrin and, of course, the women I've slept with in order to get to where I am today.

INDEX